Super Cute Girls : Coloring book for Kids

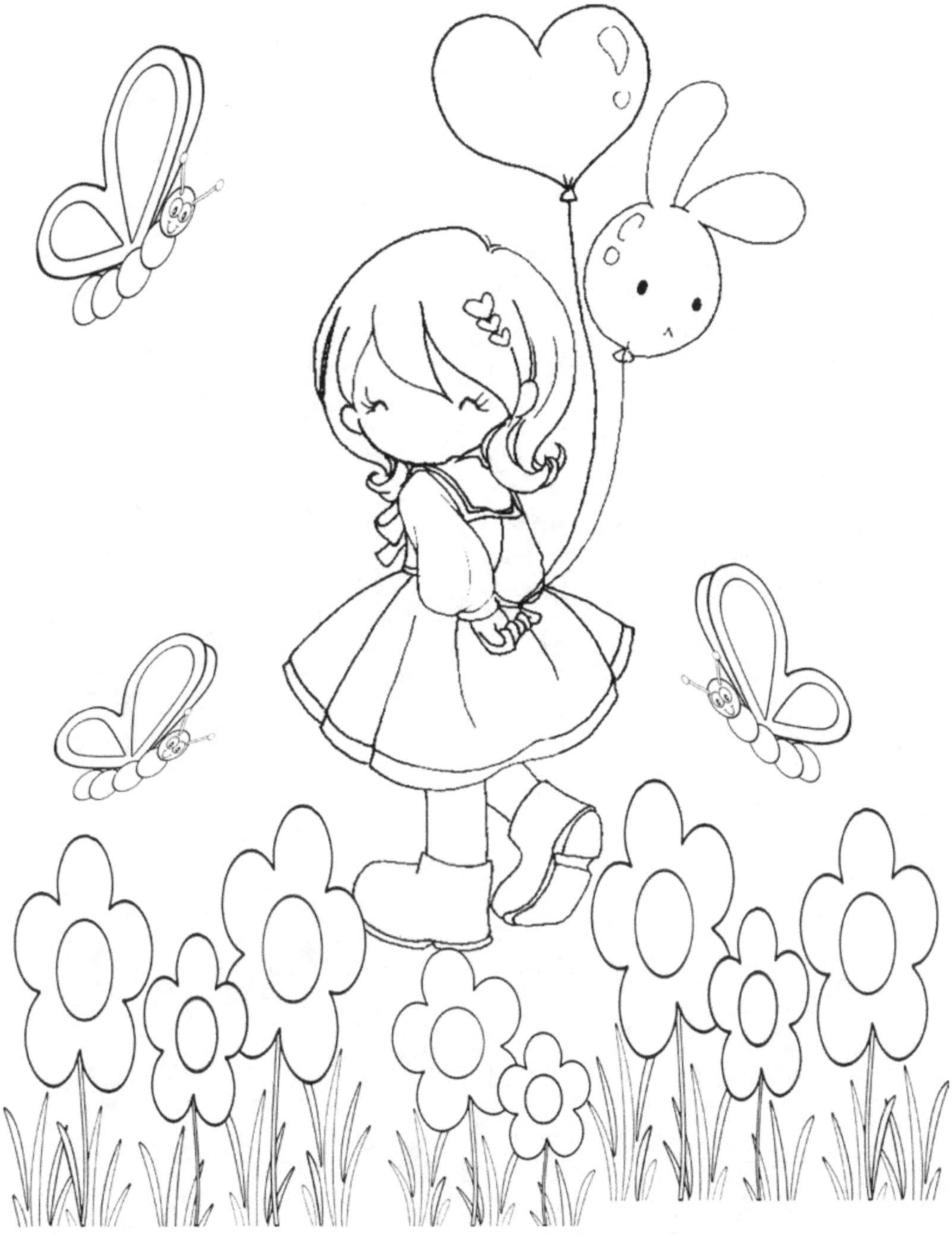

Nina Packer

Super Cute Girls
Coloring book for kids

Copyright: Published in the United States by Nina Packer
Published February 2018

All rights reserved. No part of this publication may be reproduced, stored in retrieval system, copied in any form or by any means, electronic, mechanical, photocopying, recording or otherwise transmitted without written permission from the publisher. Please do not participate in or encourage piracy of this material in any way. You must not circulate this book in any format Nina Packer does not control or direct users' actions and is not responsible for the information or content shared, harm and/or actions of the book readers.

ISBN-13: 978-1984980687

ISBN-10: 1984980688

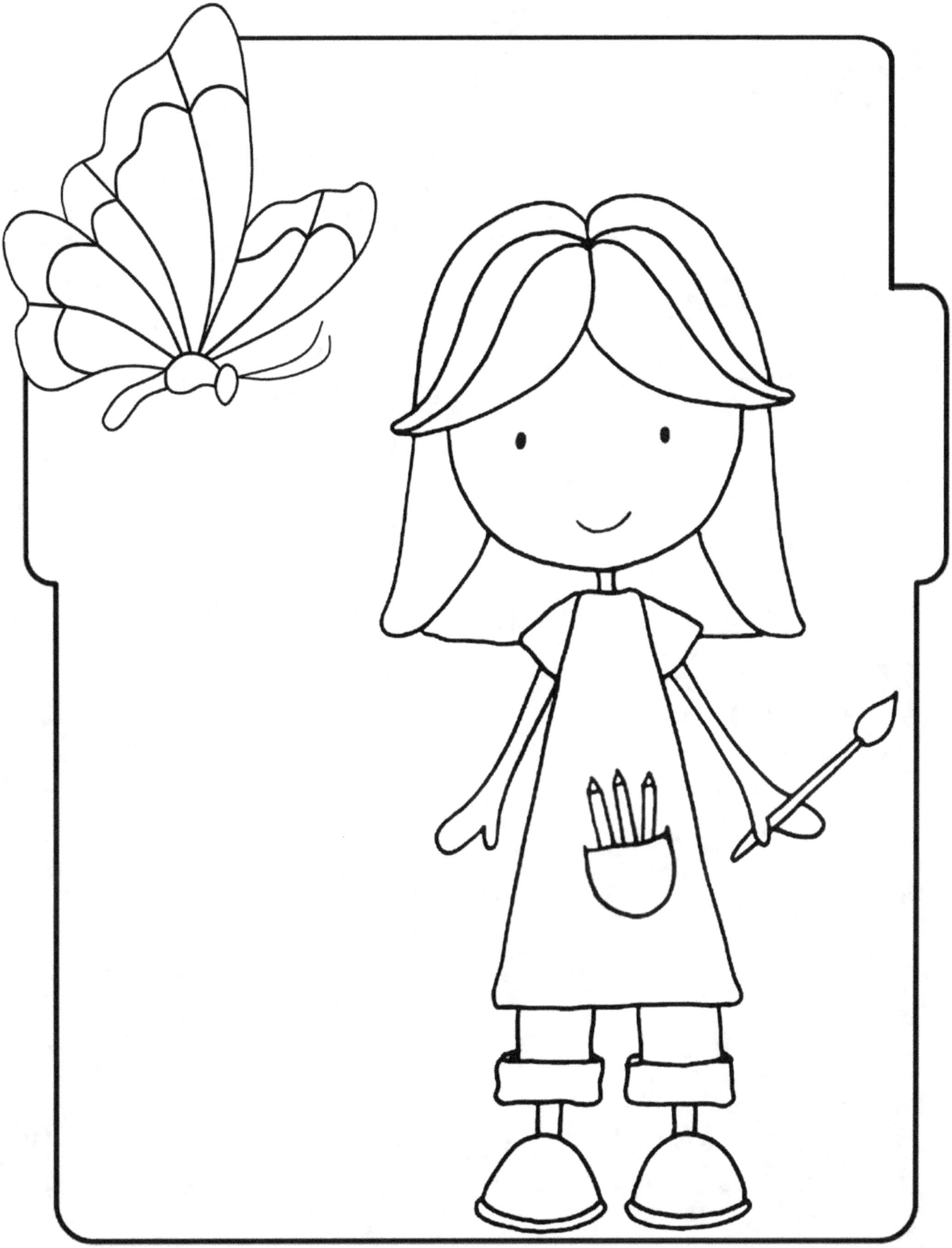

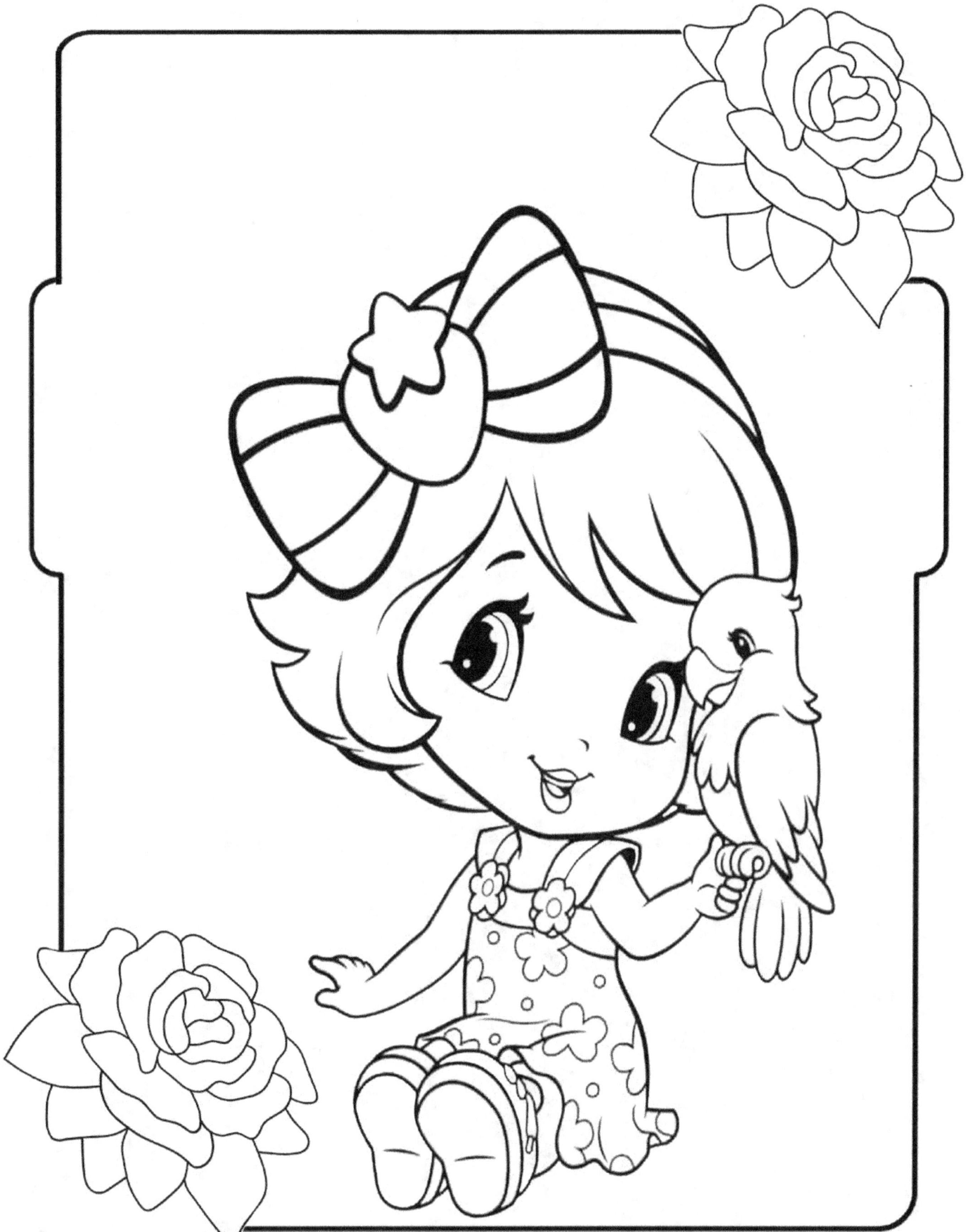

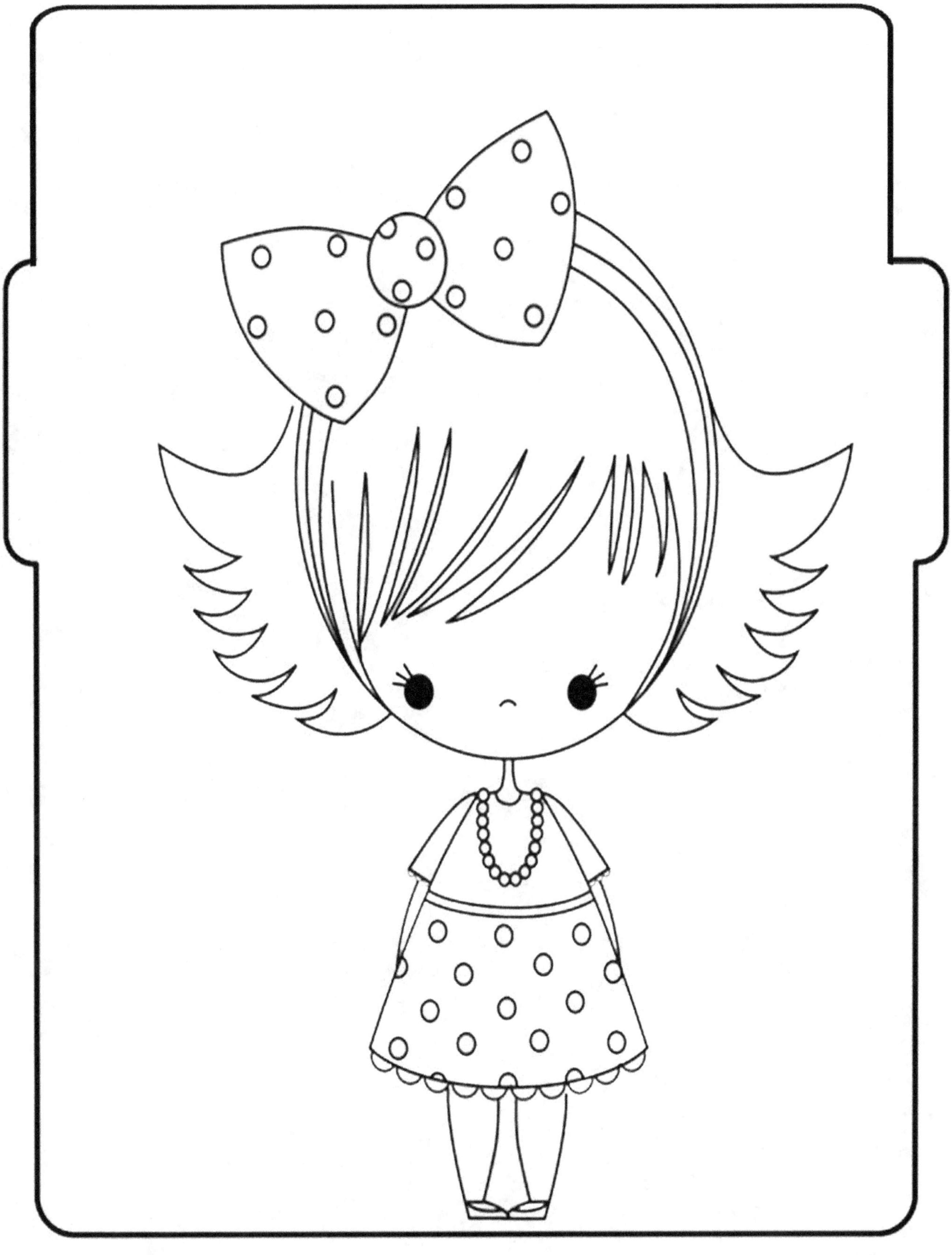

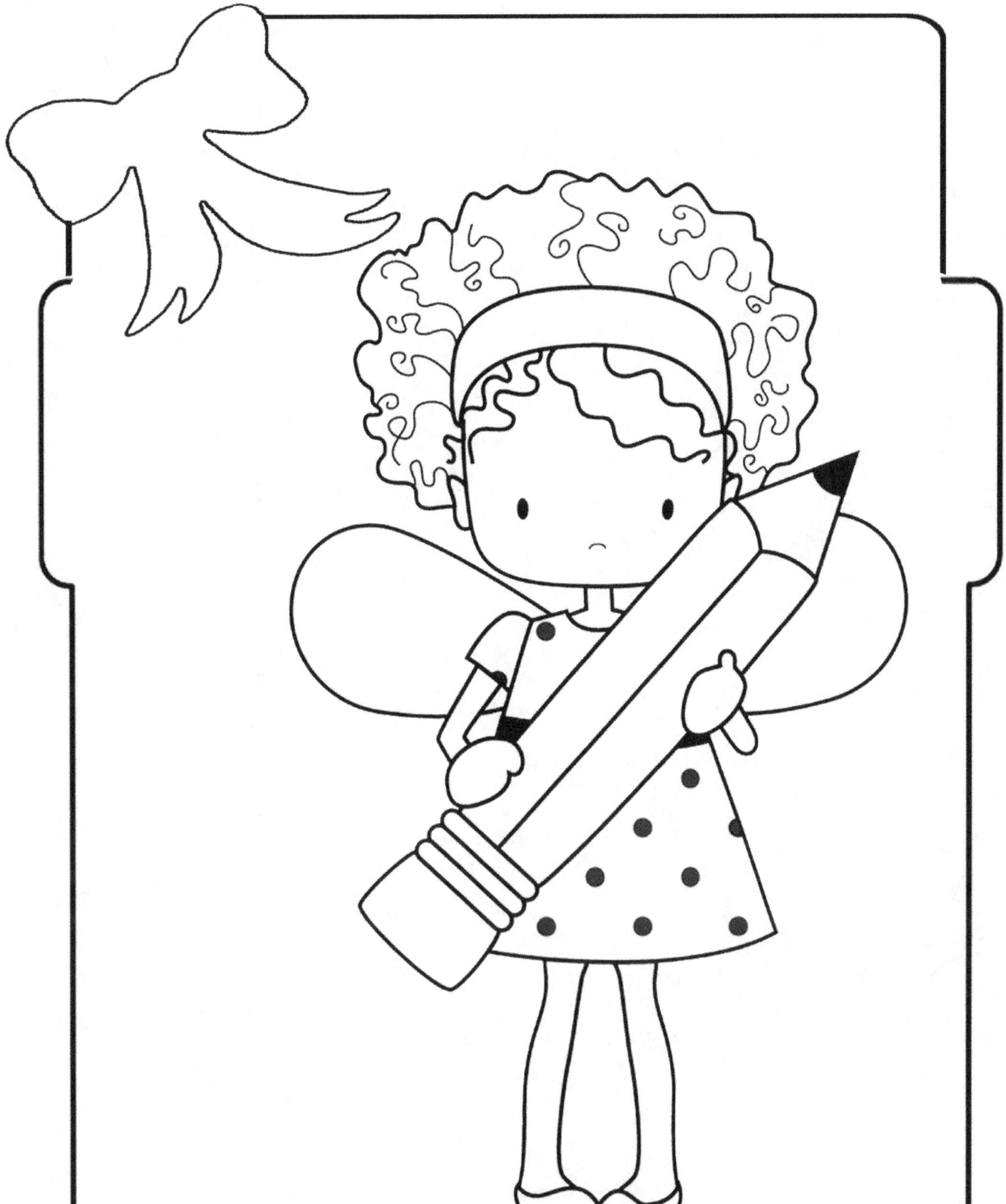

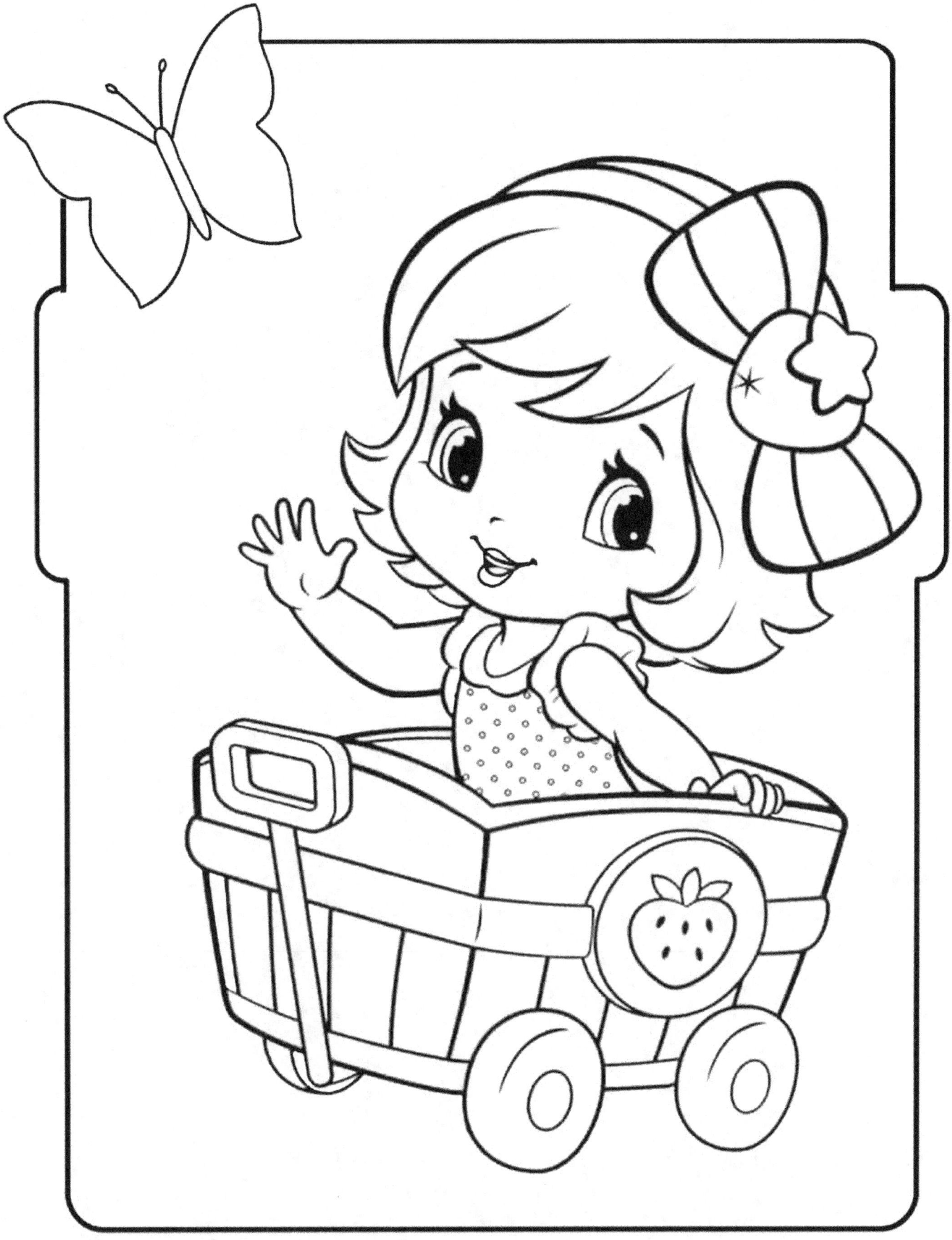

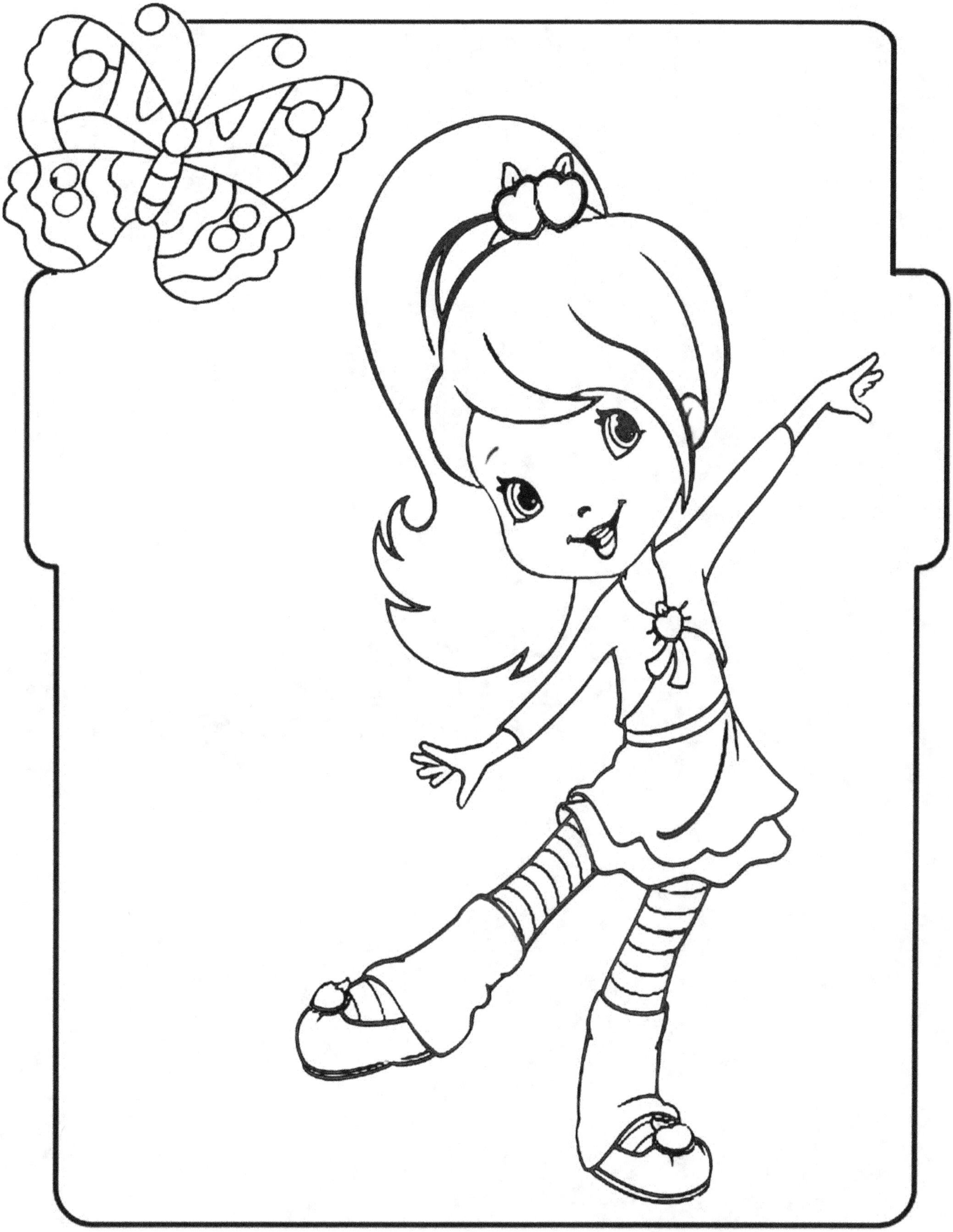

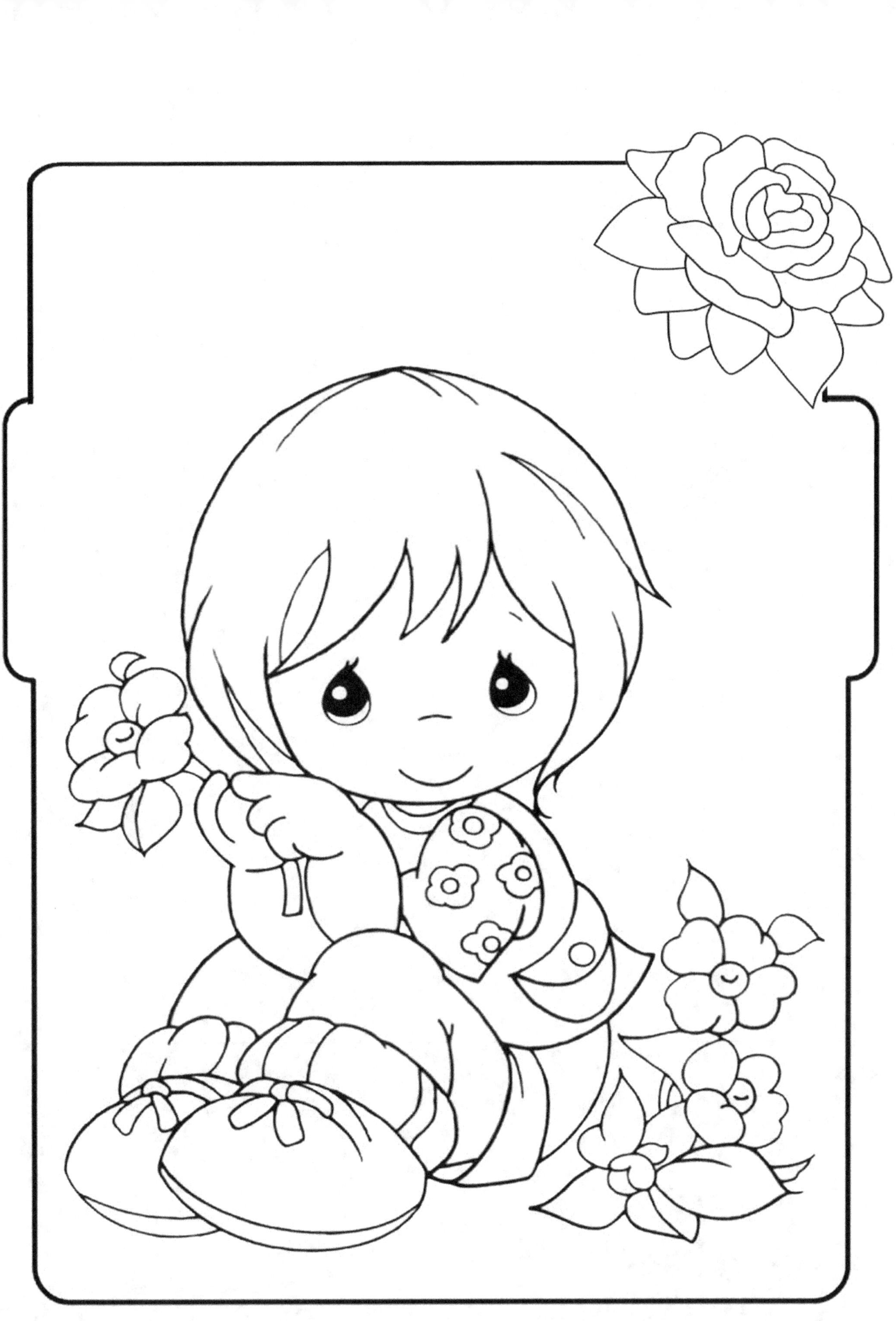

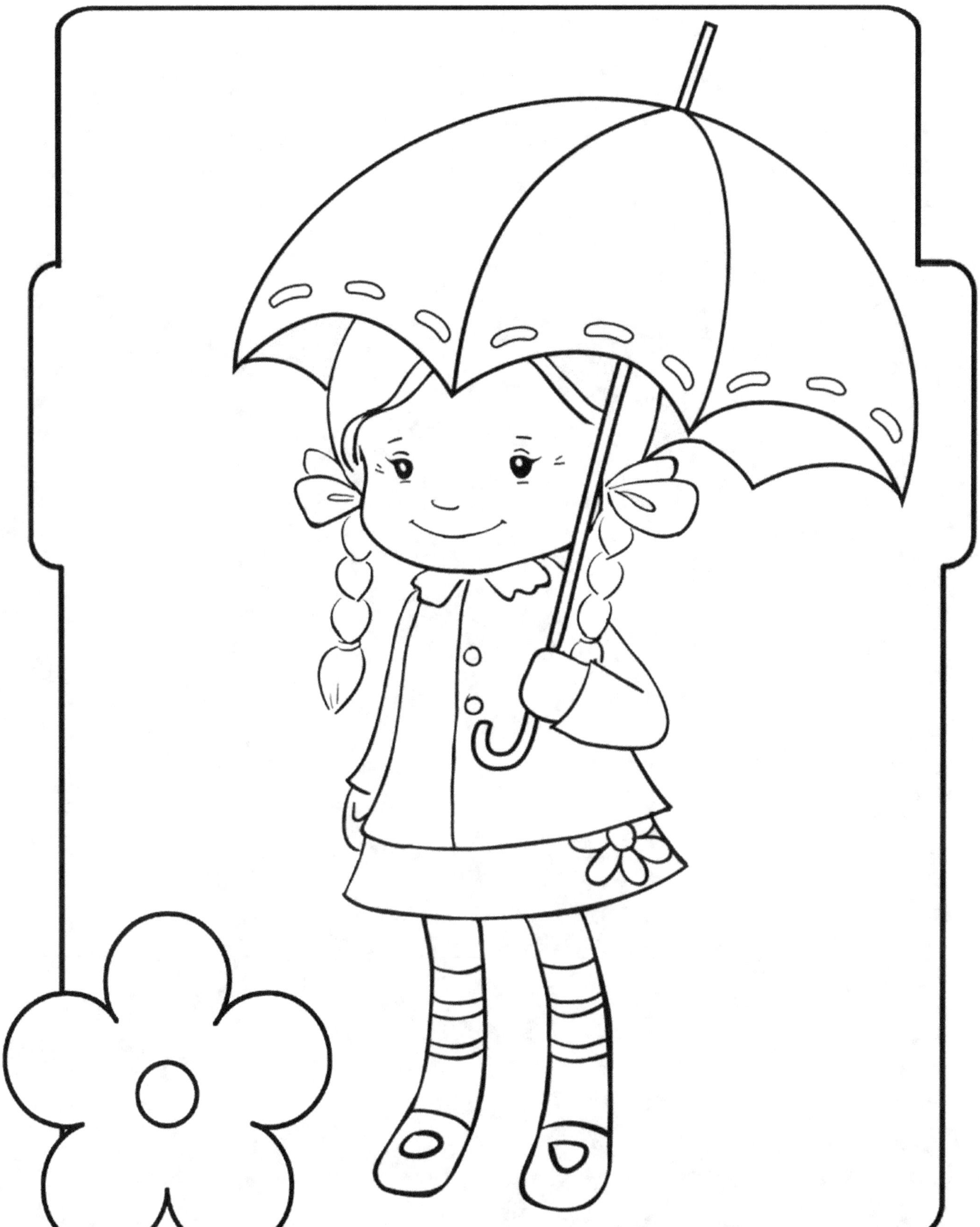

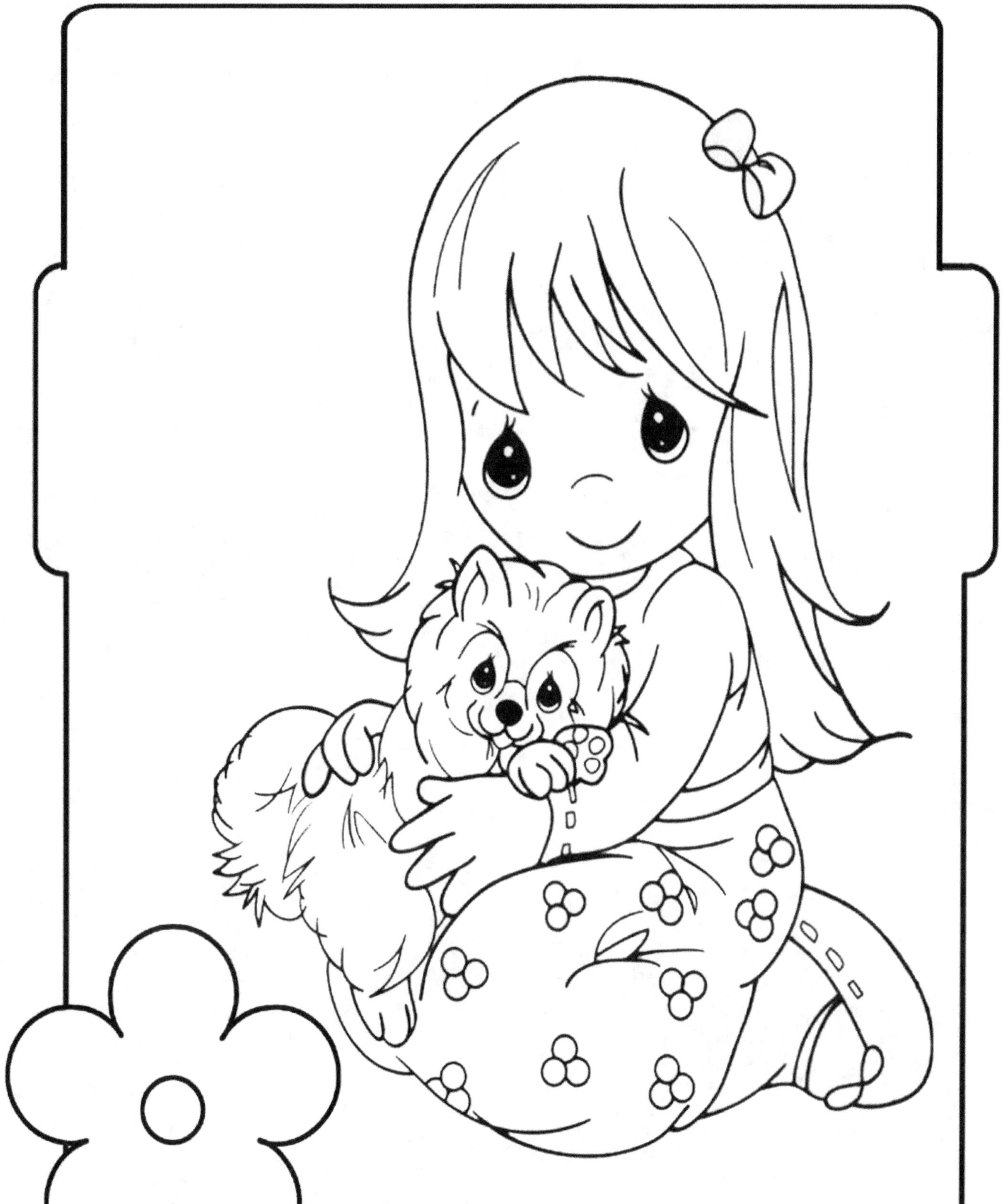

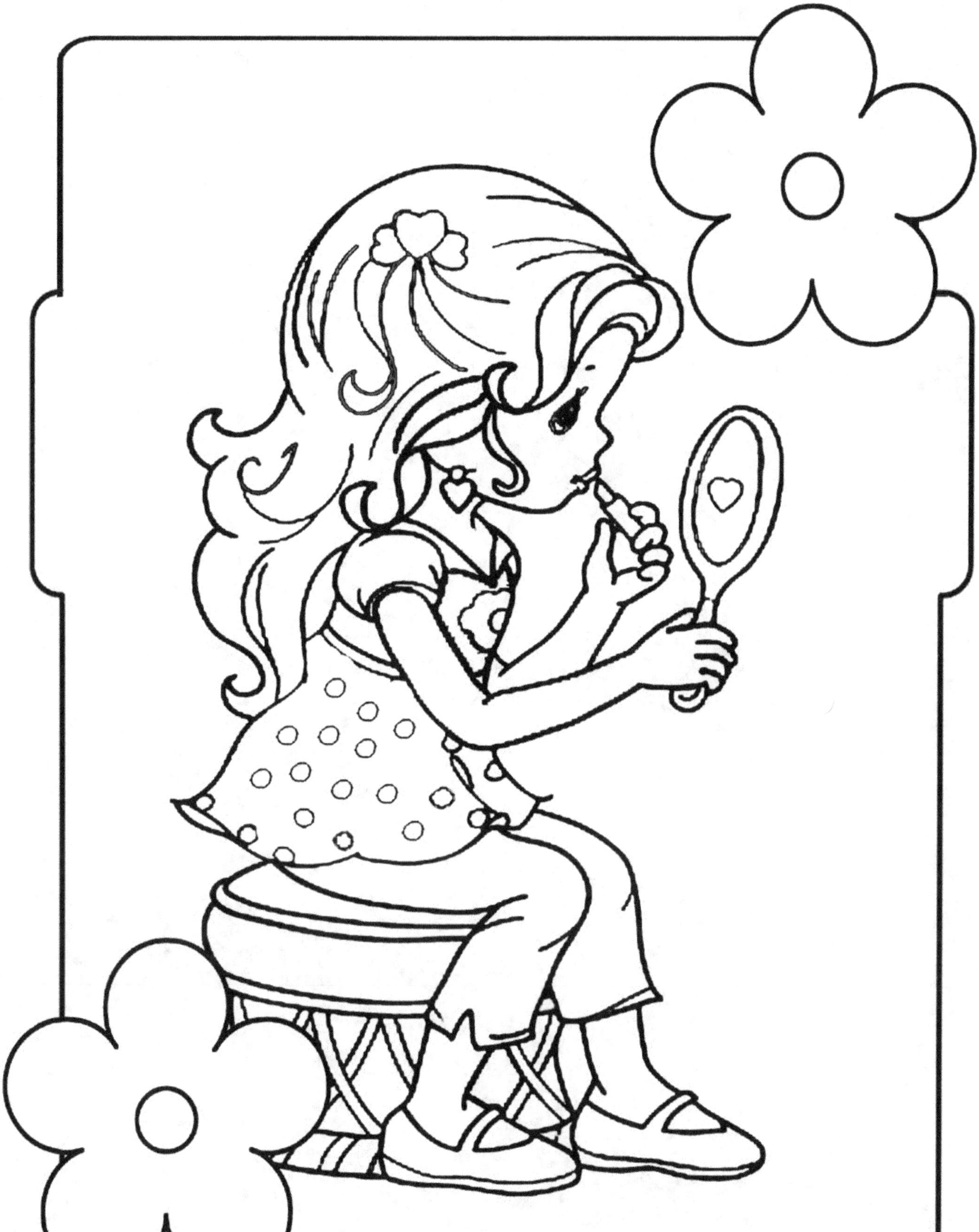

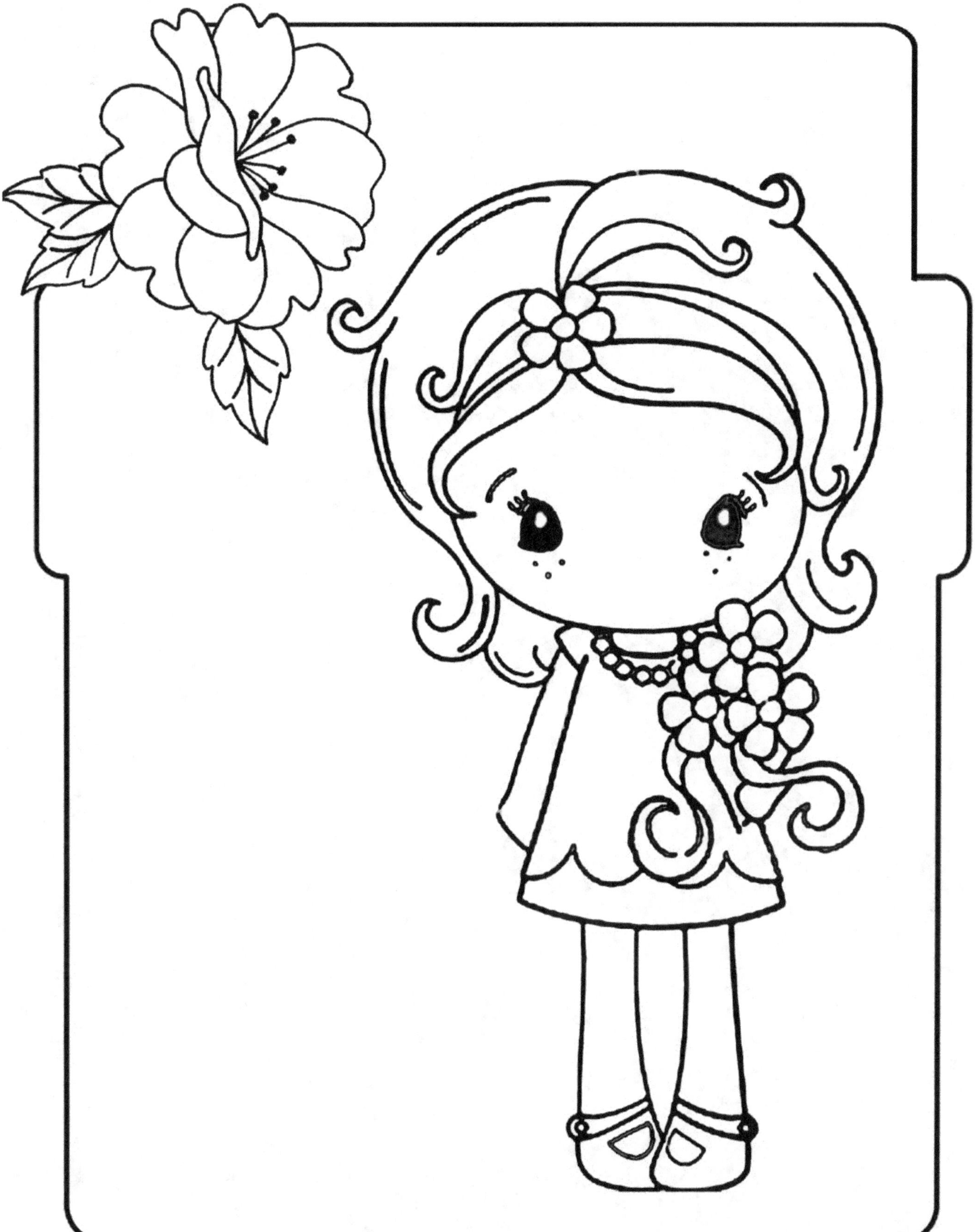

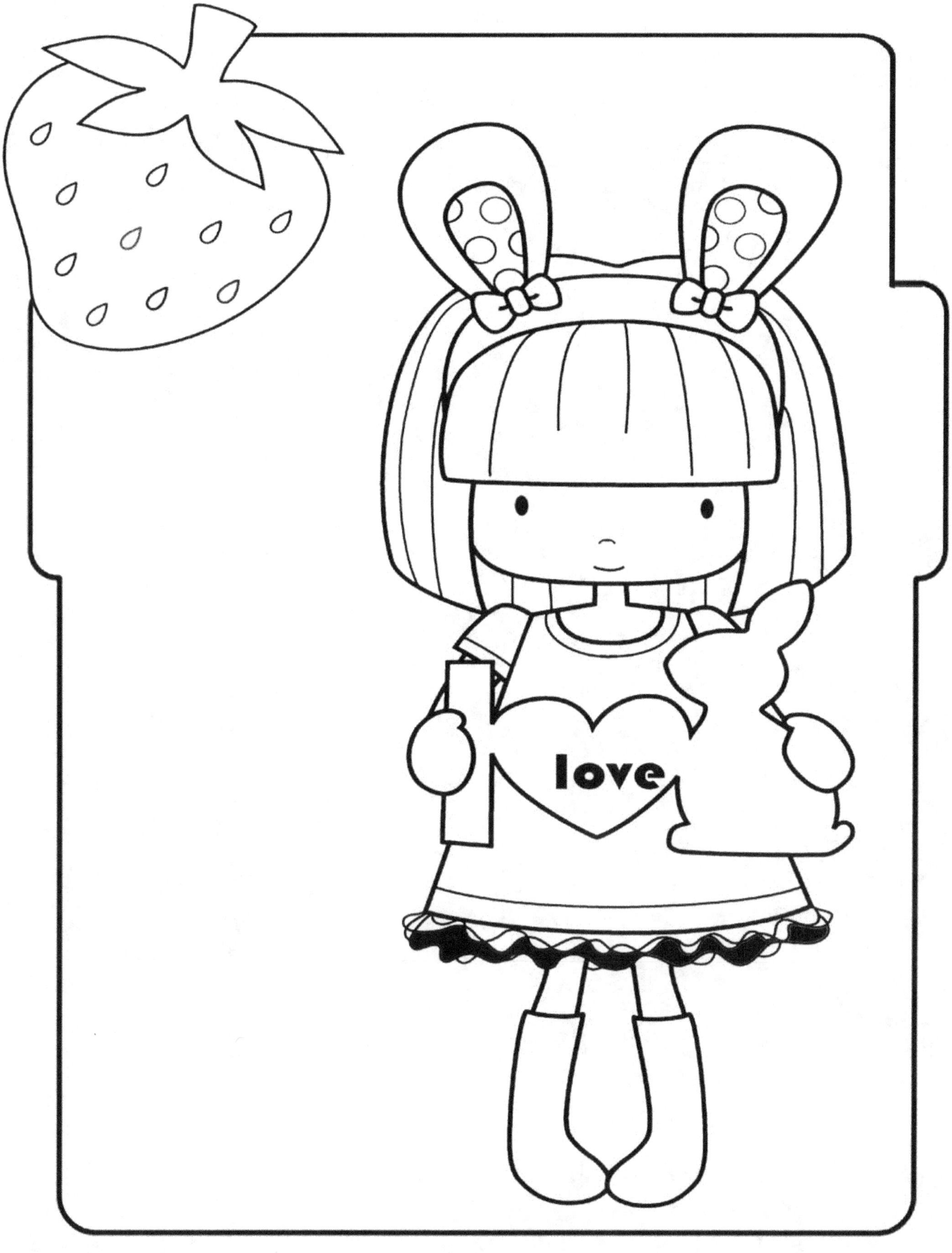
love

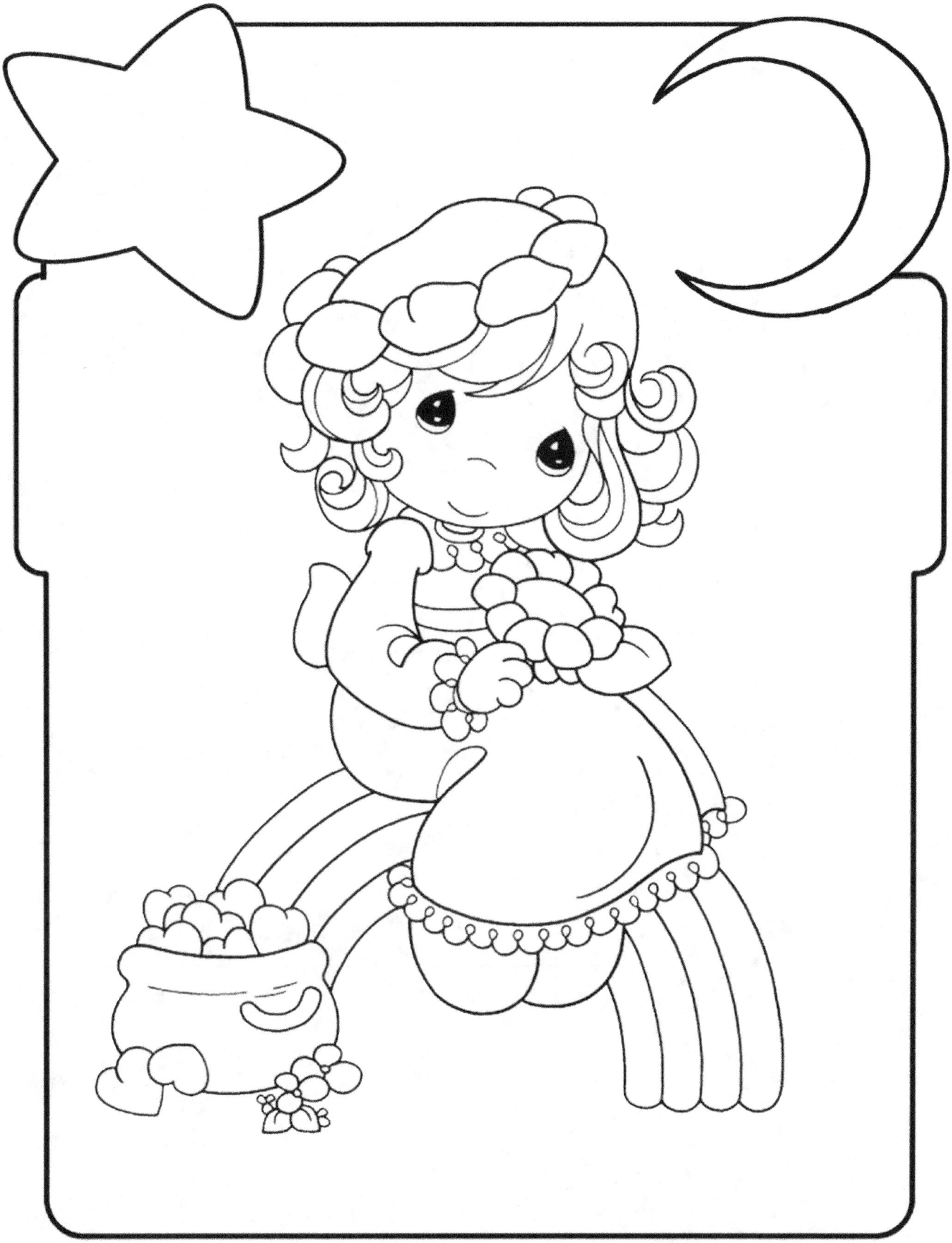

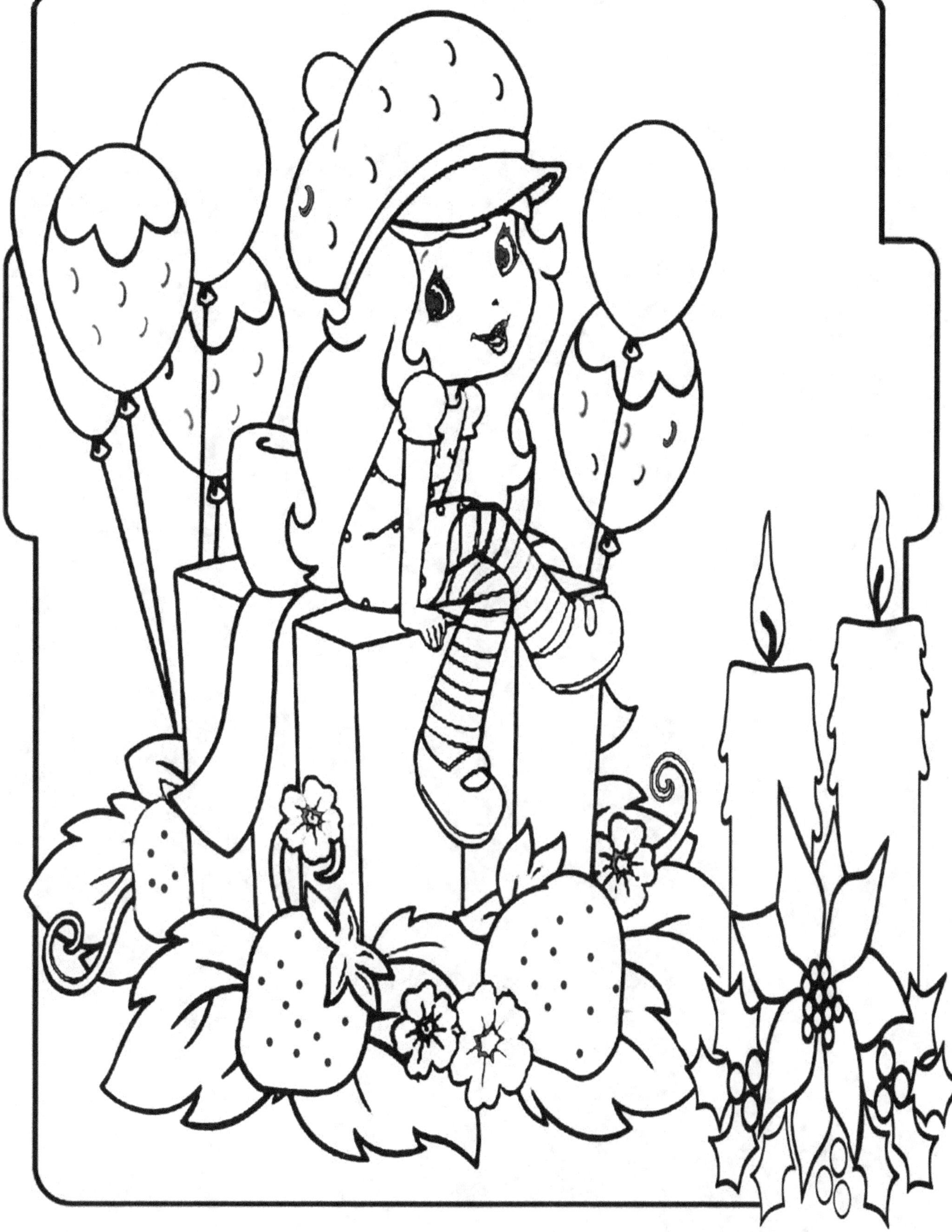

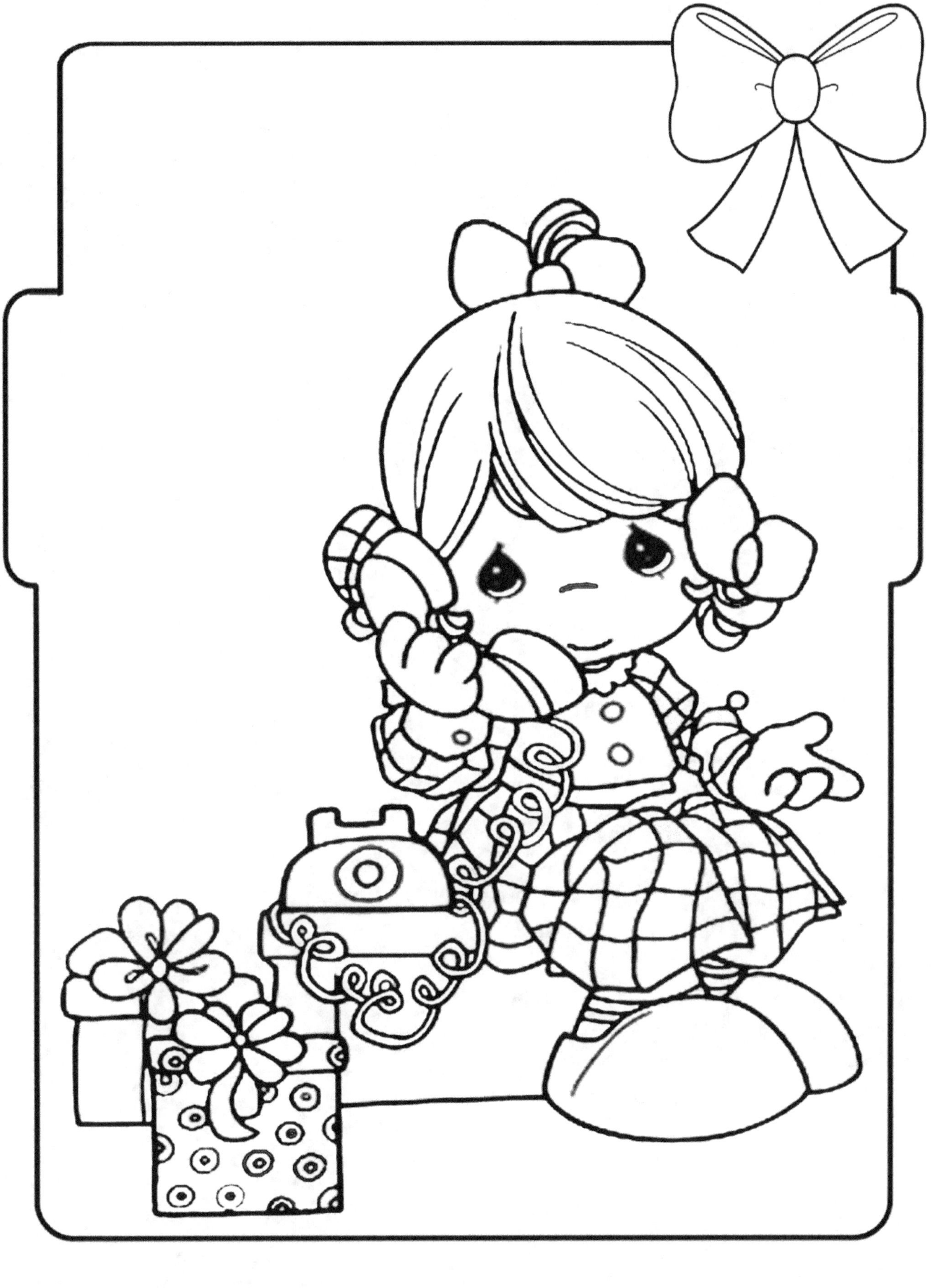

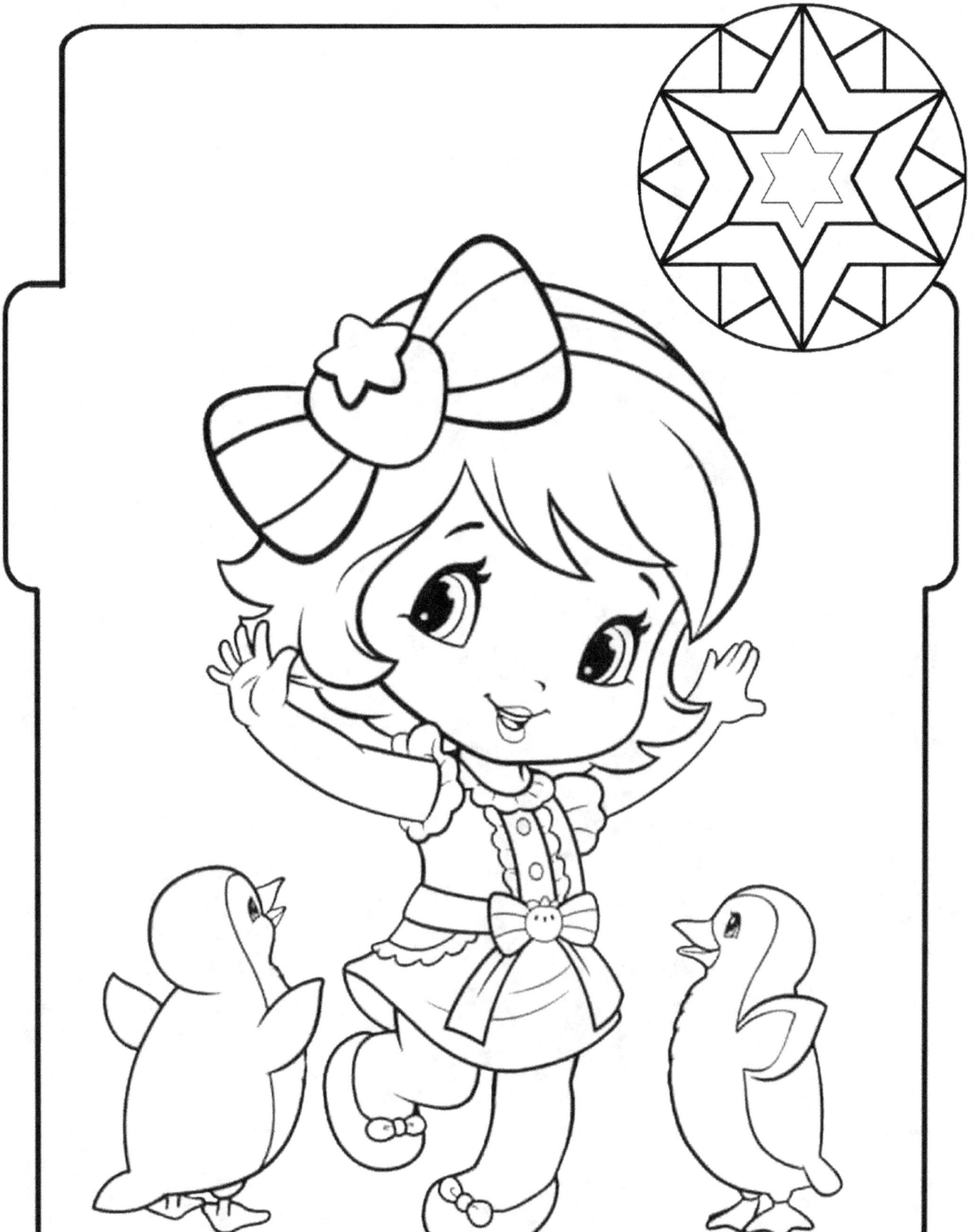

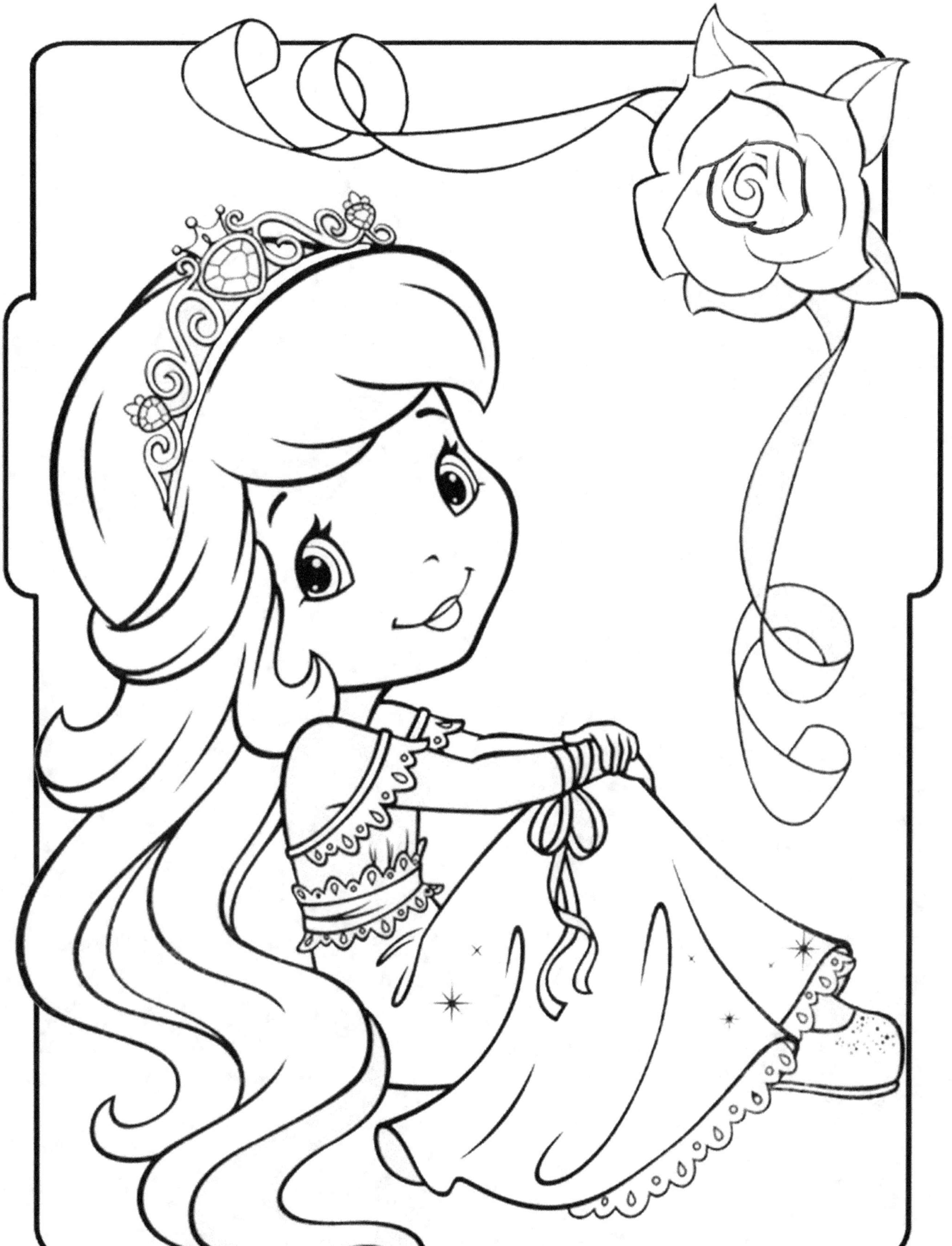

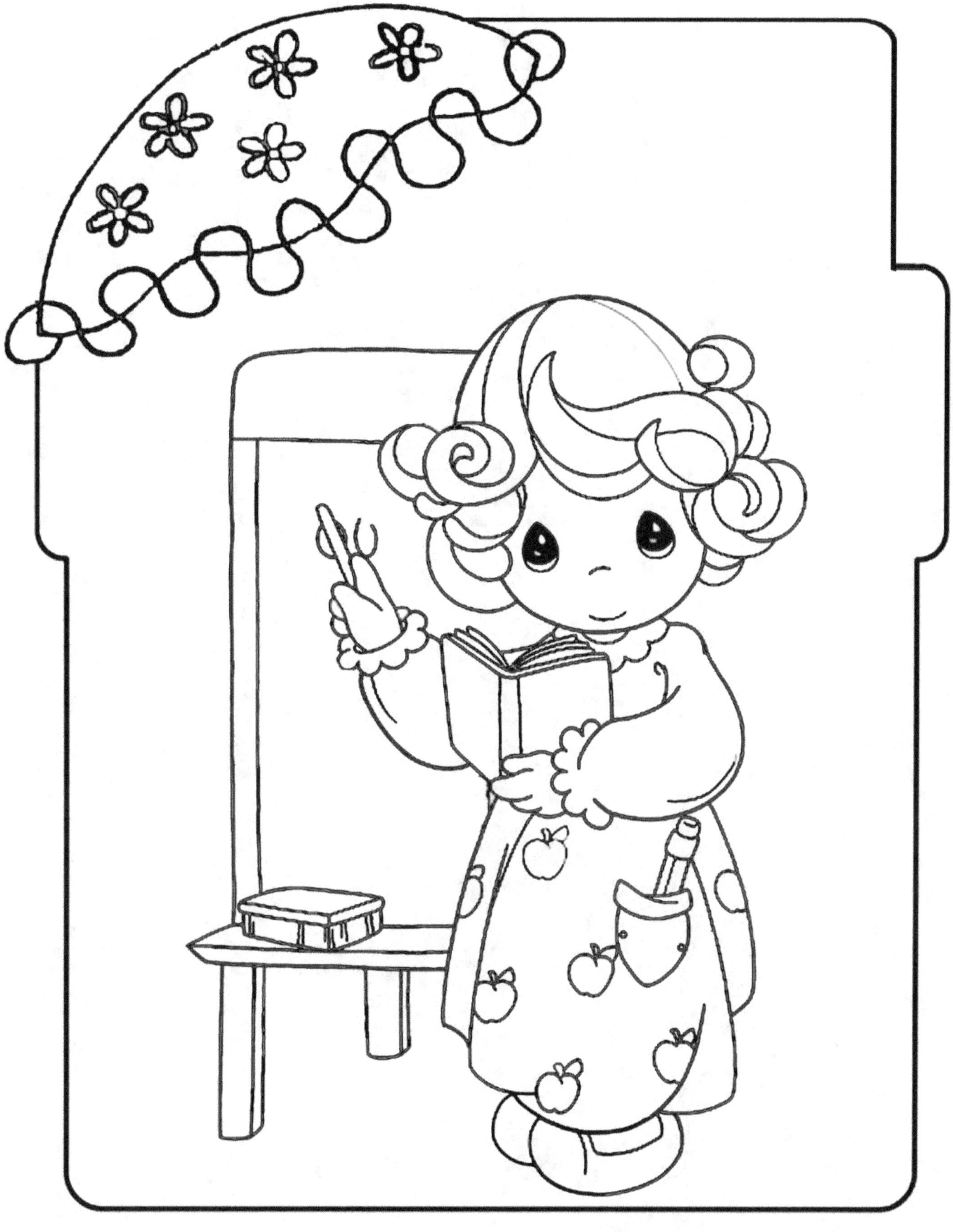

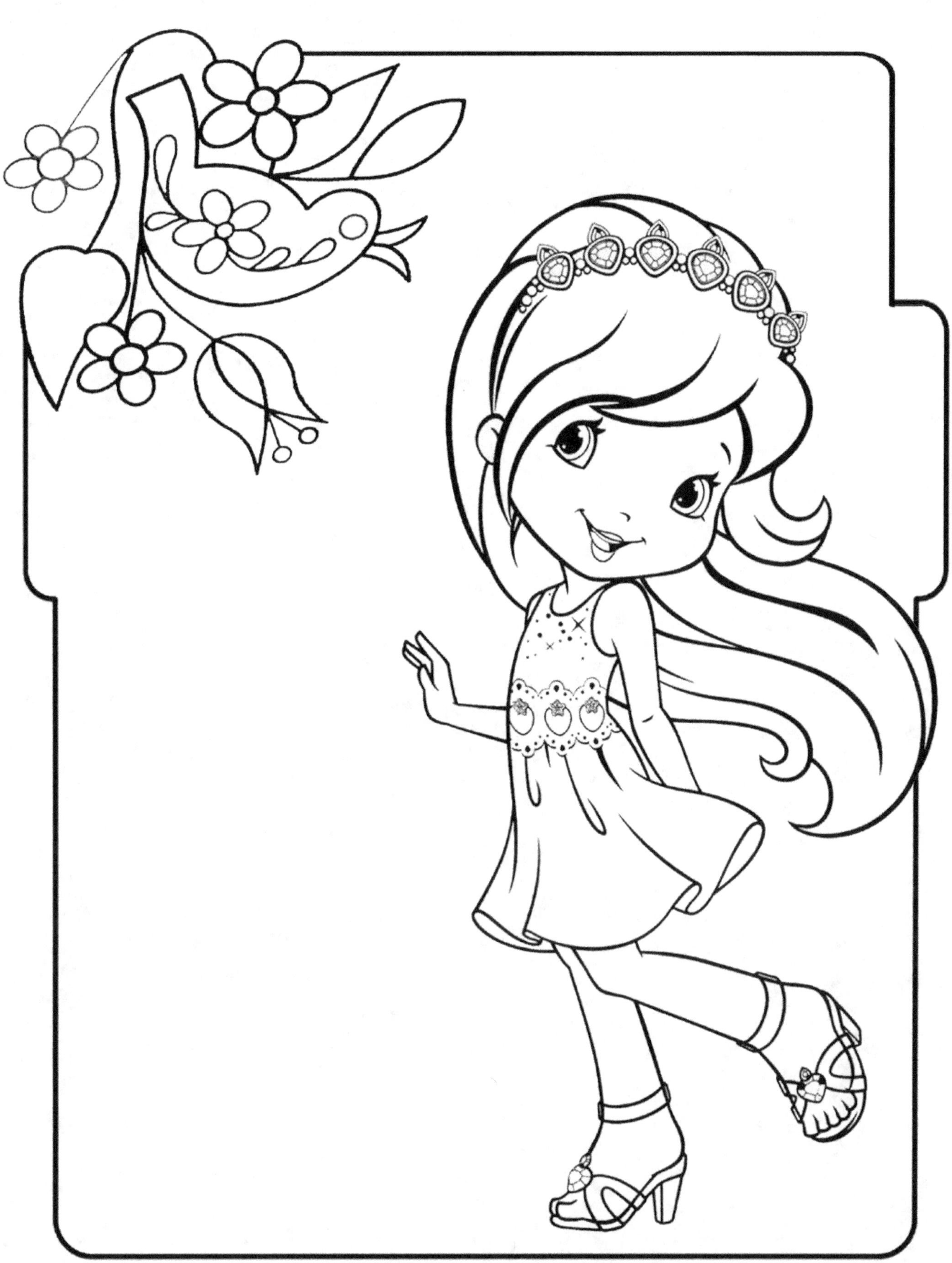

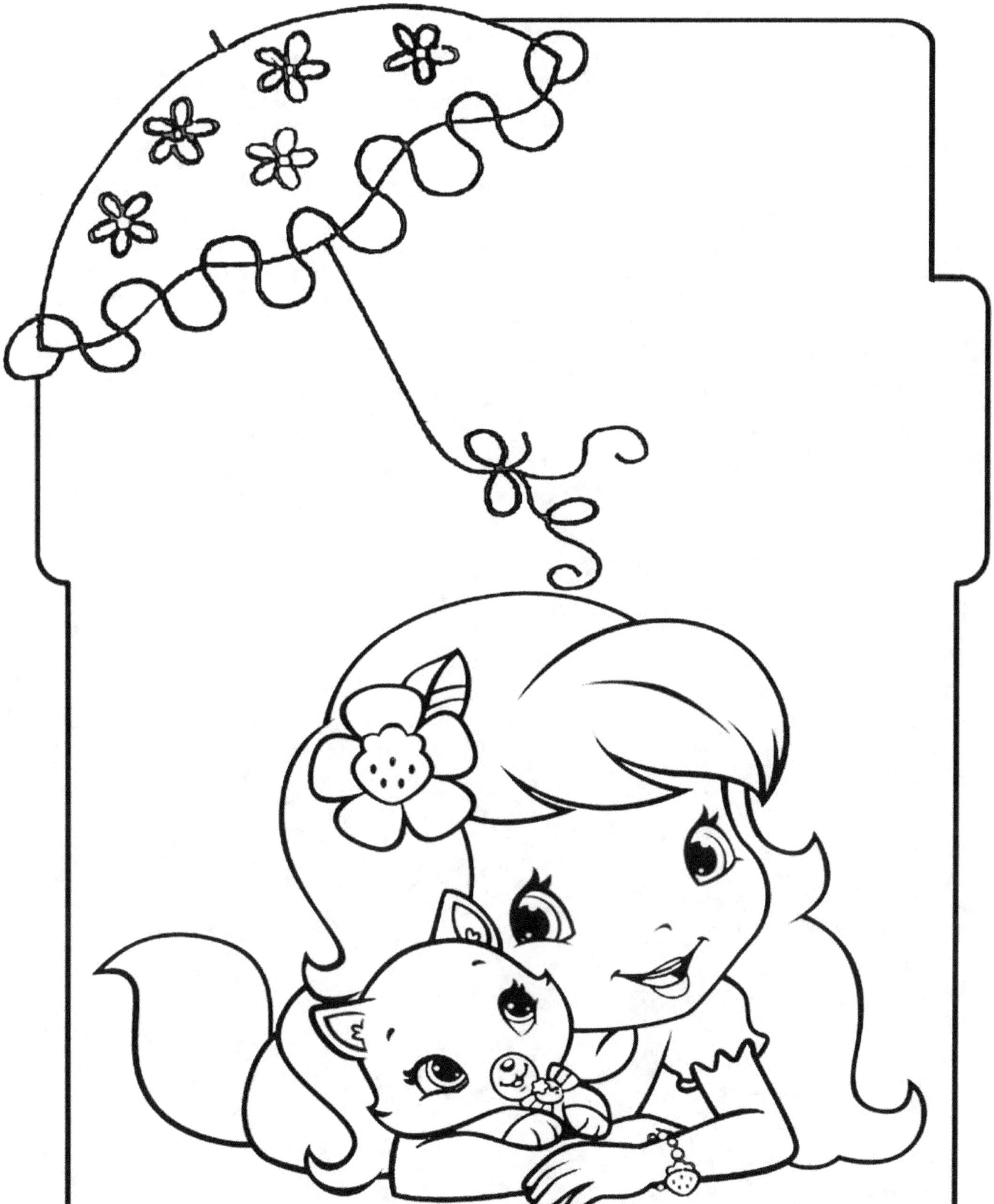

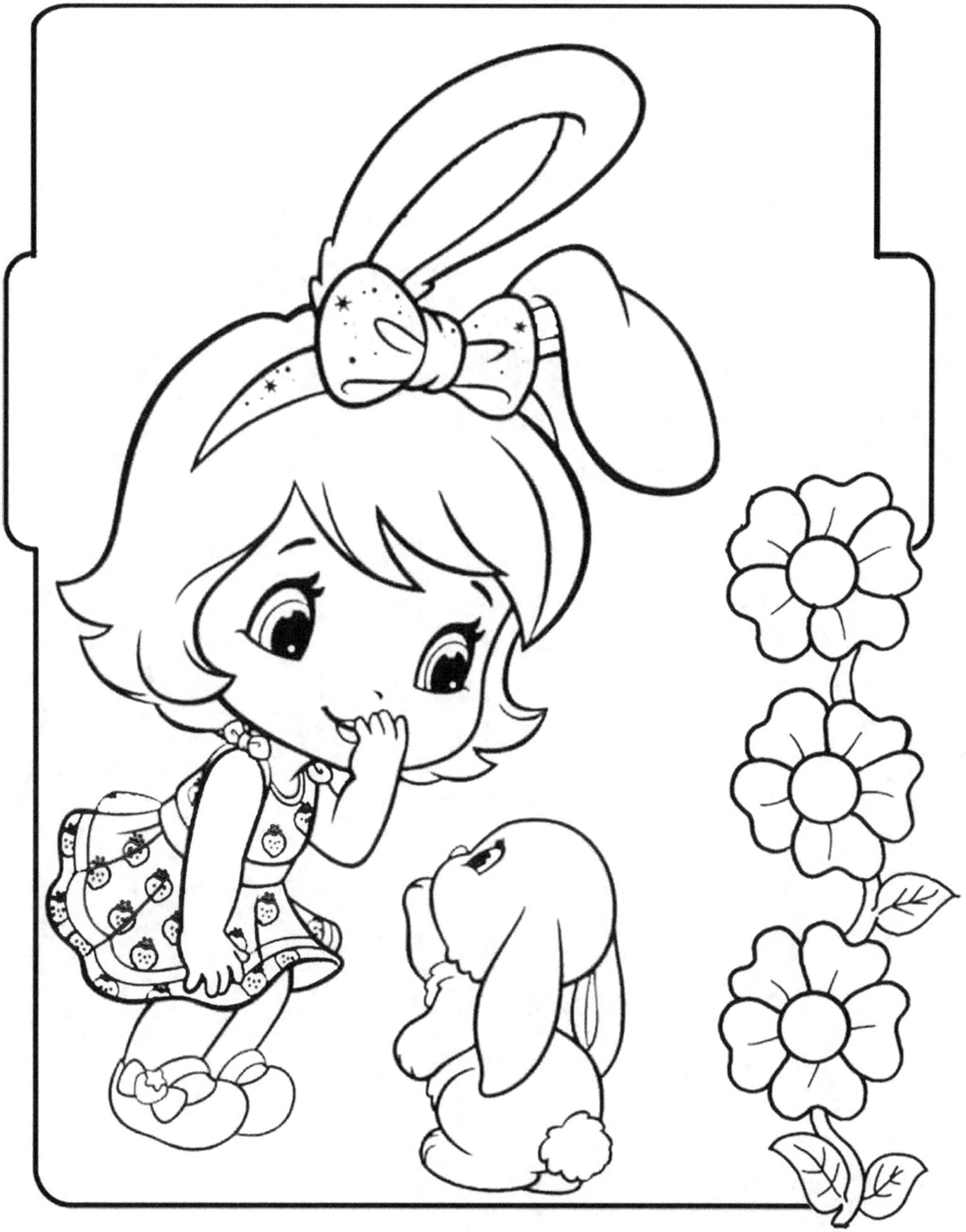

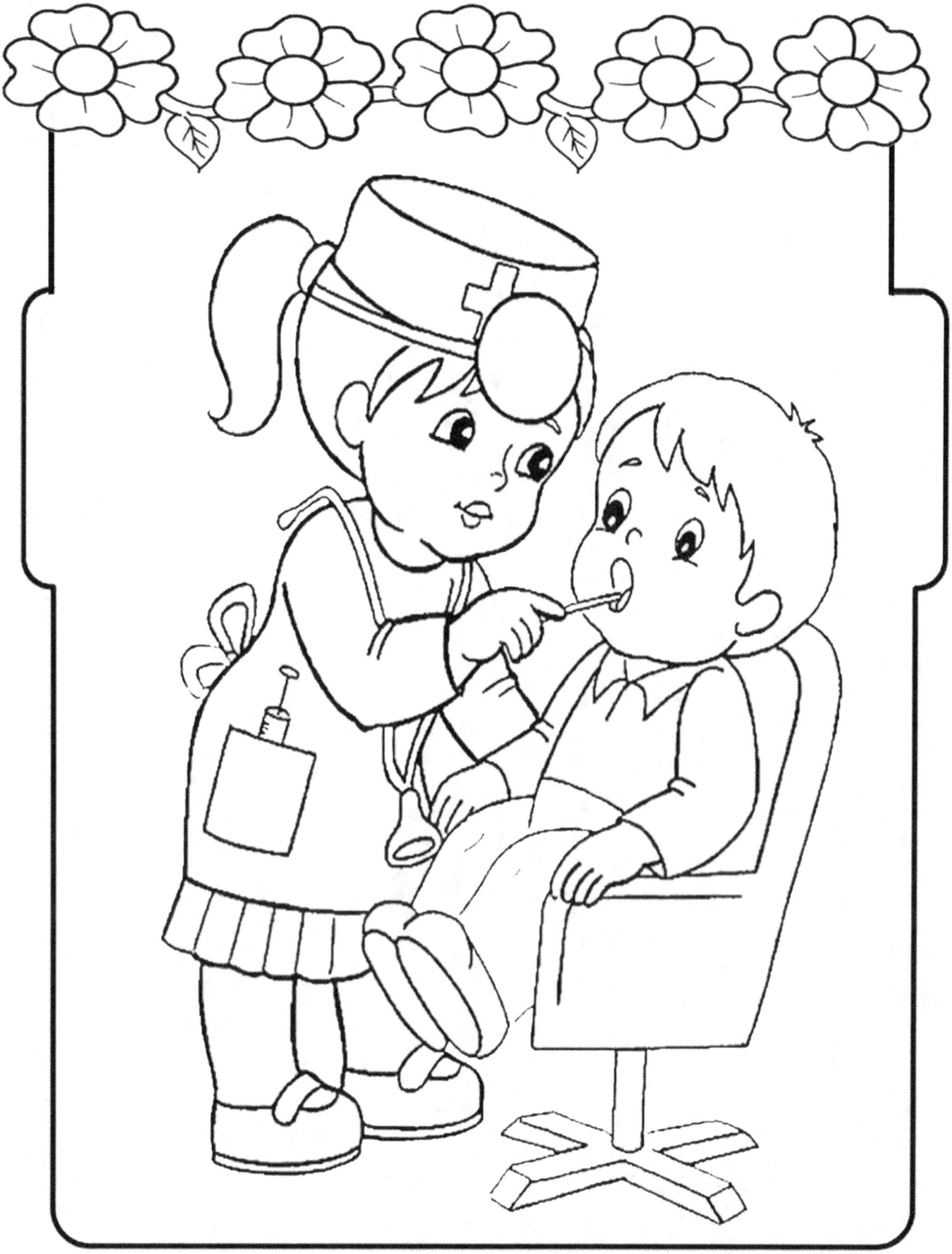

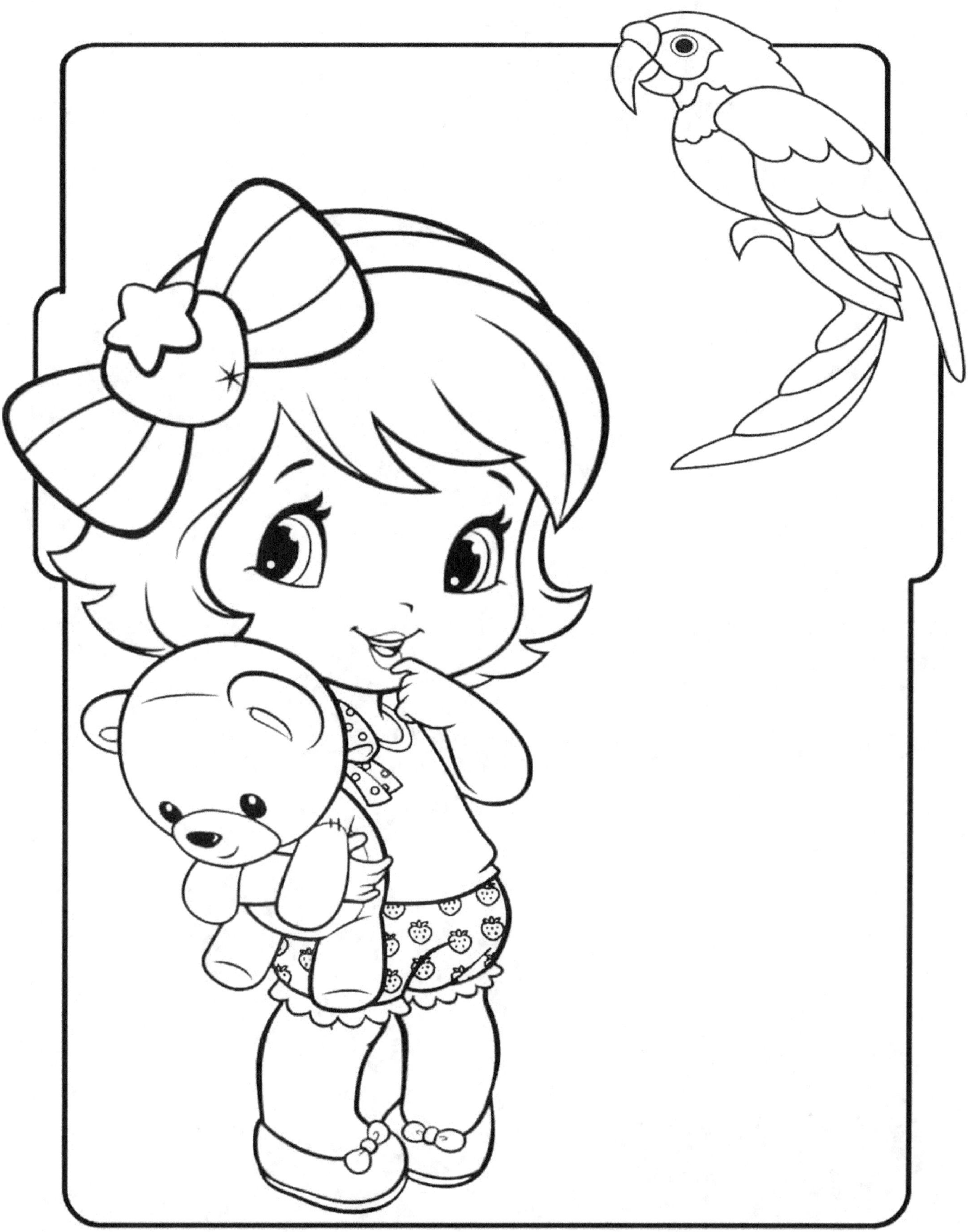

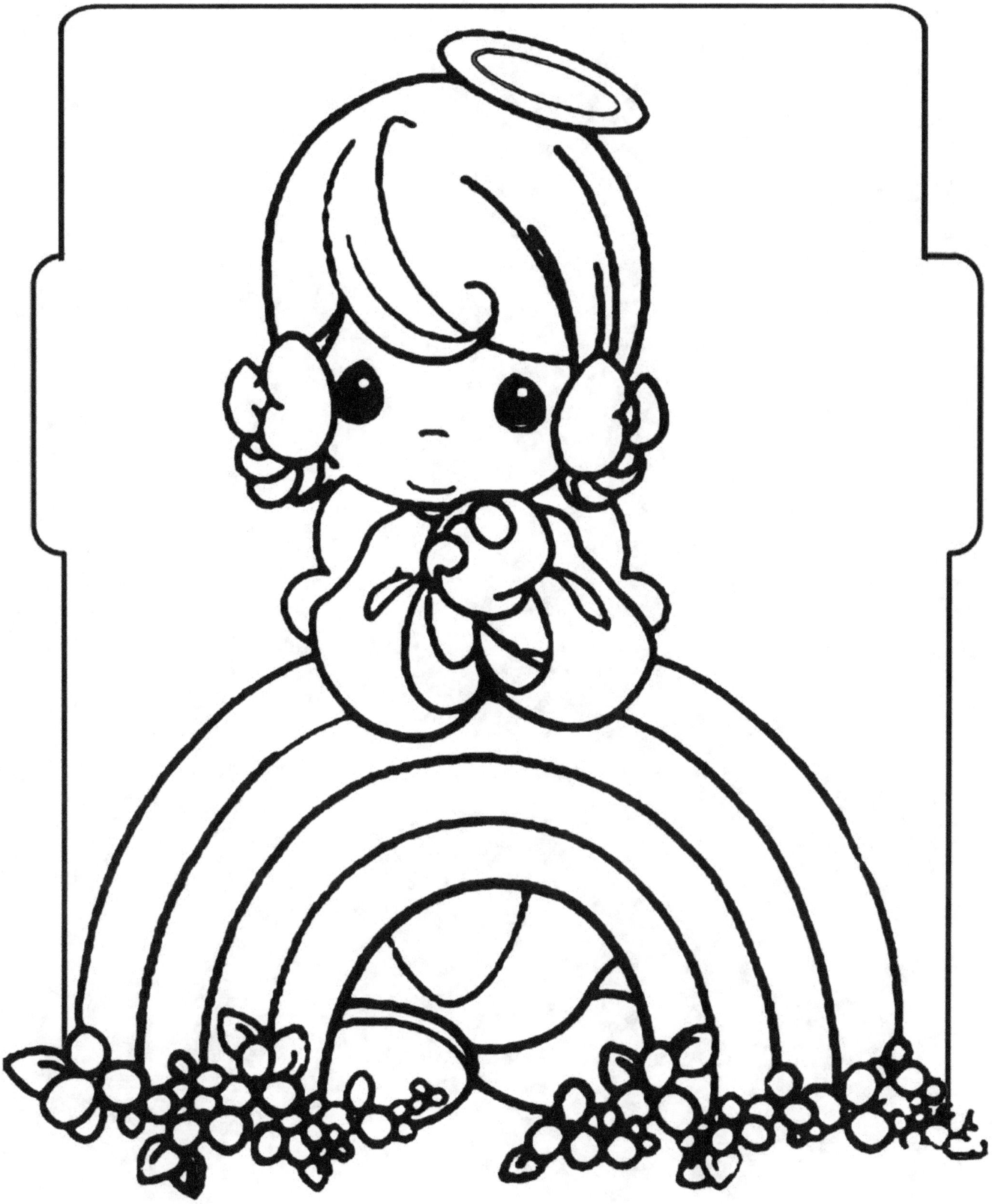

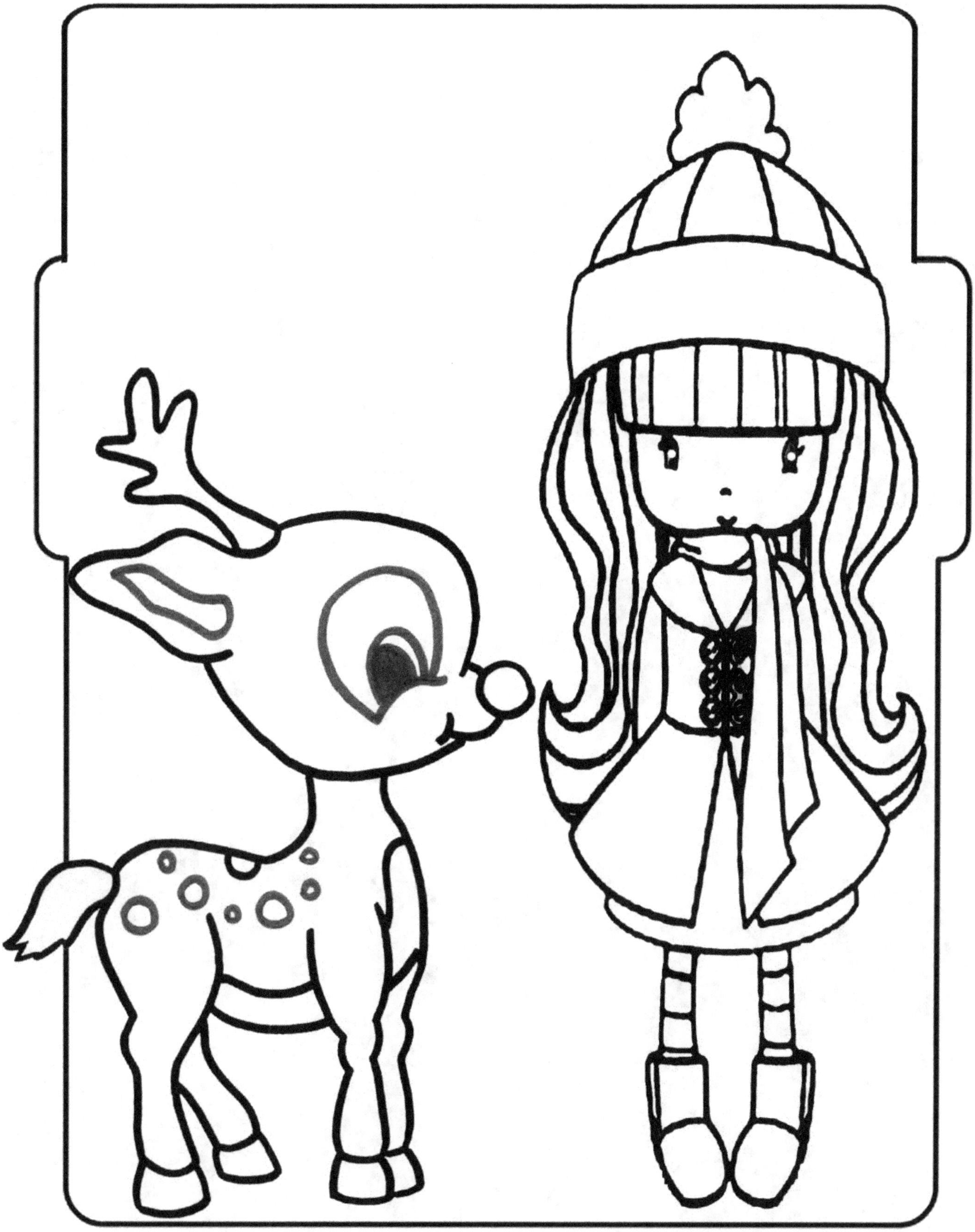

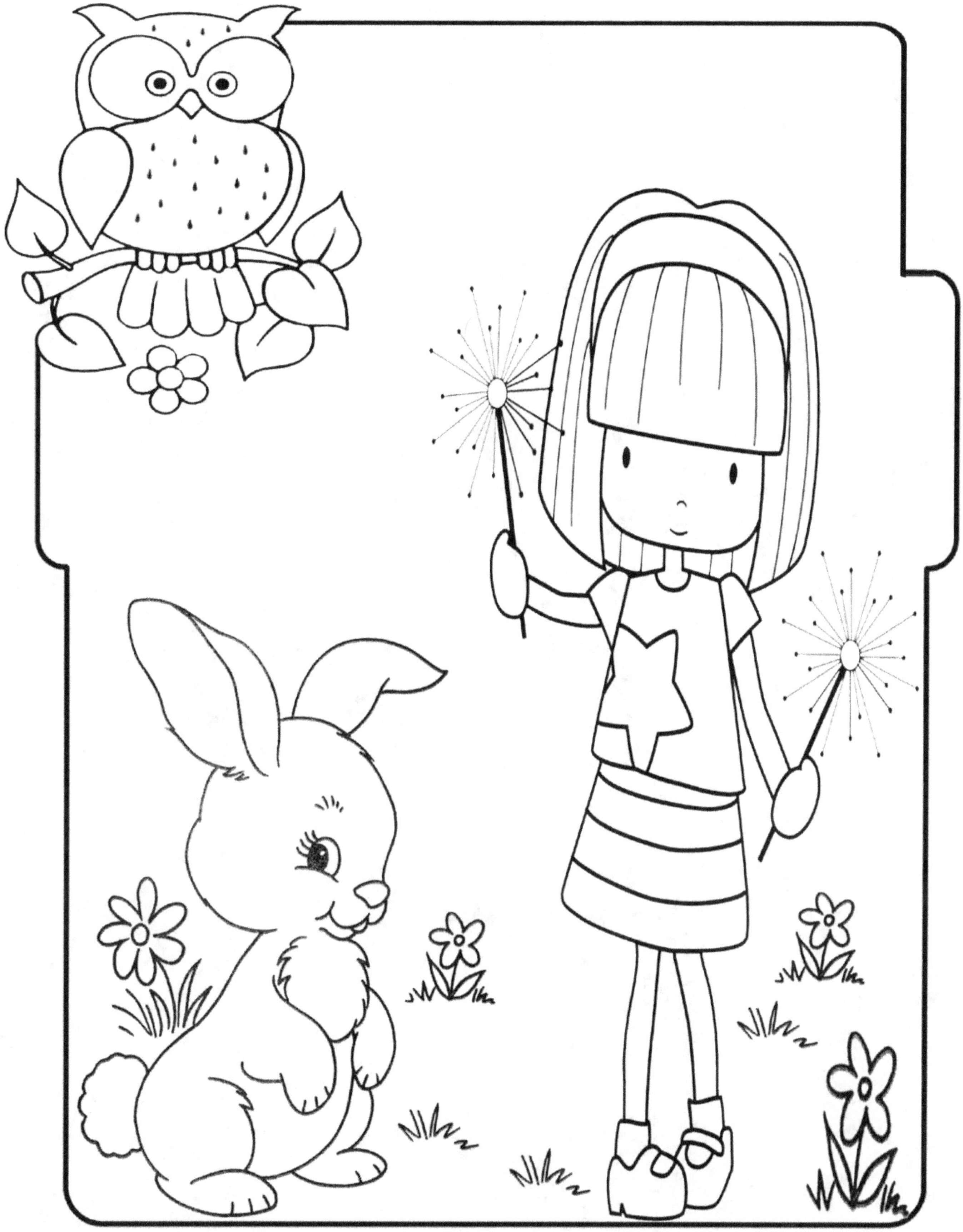

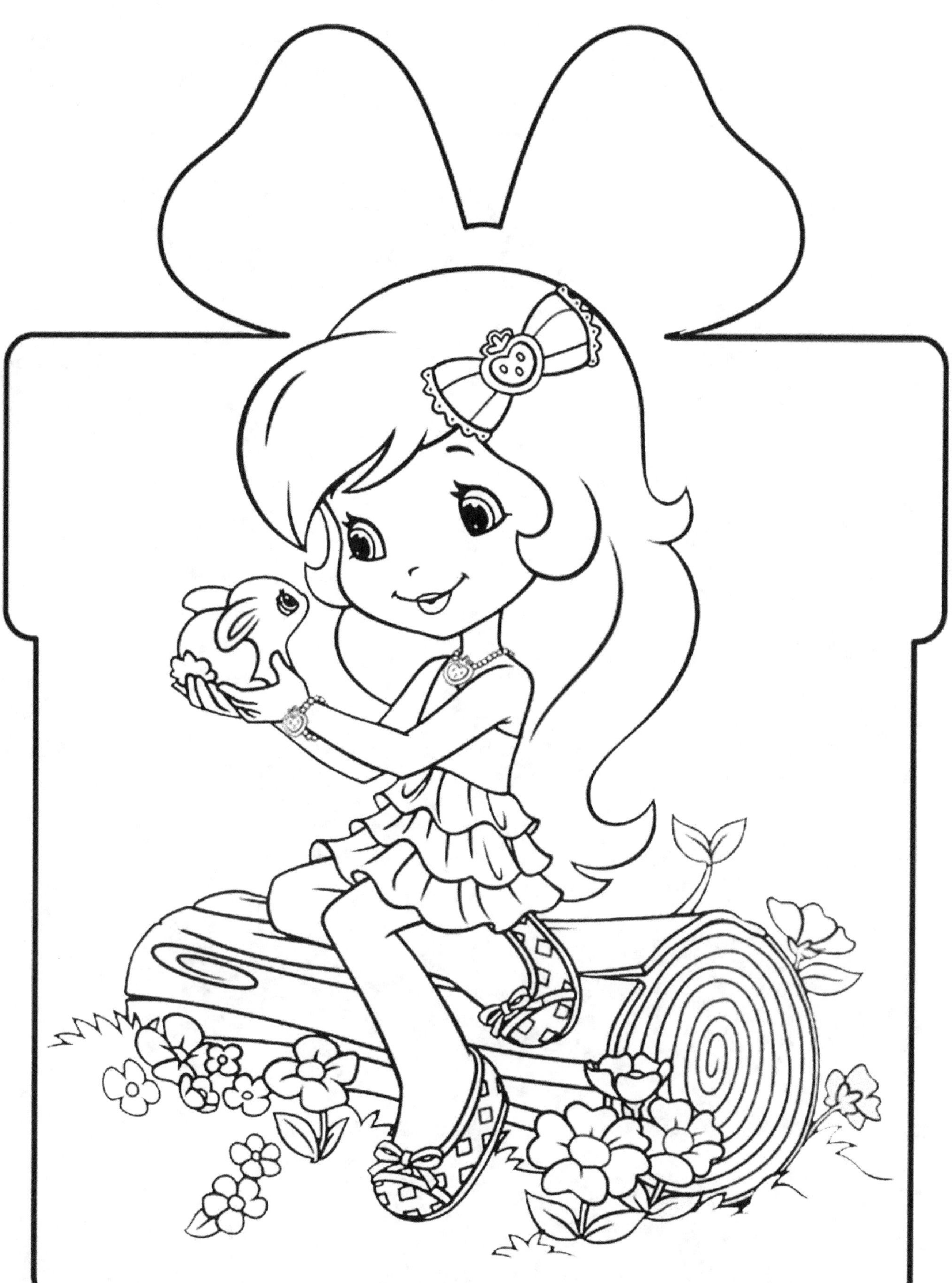

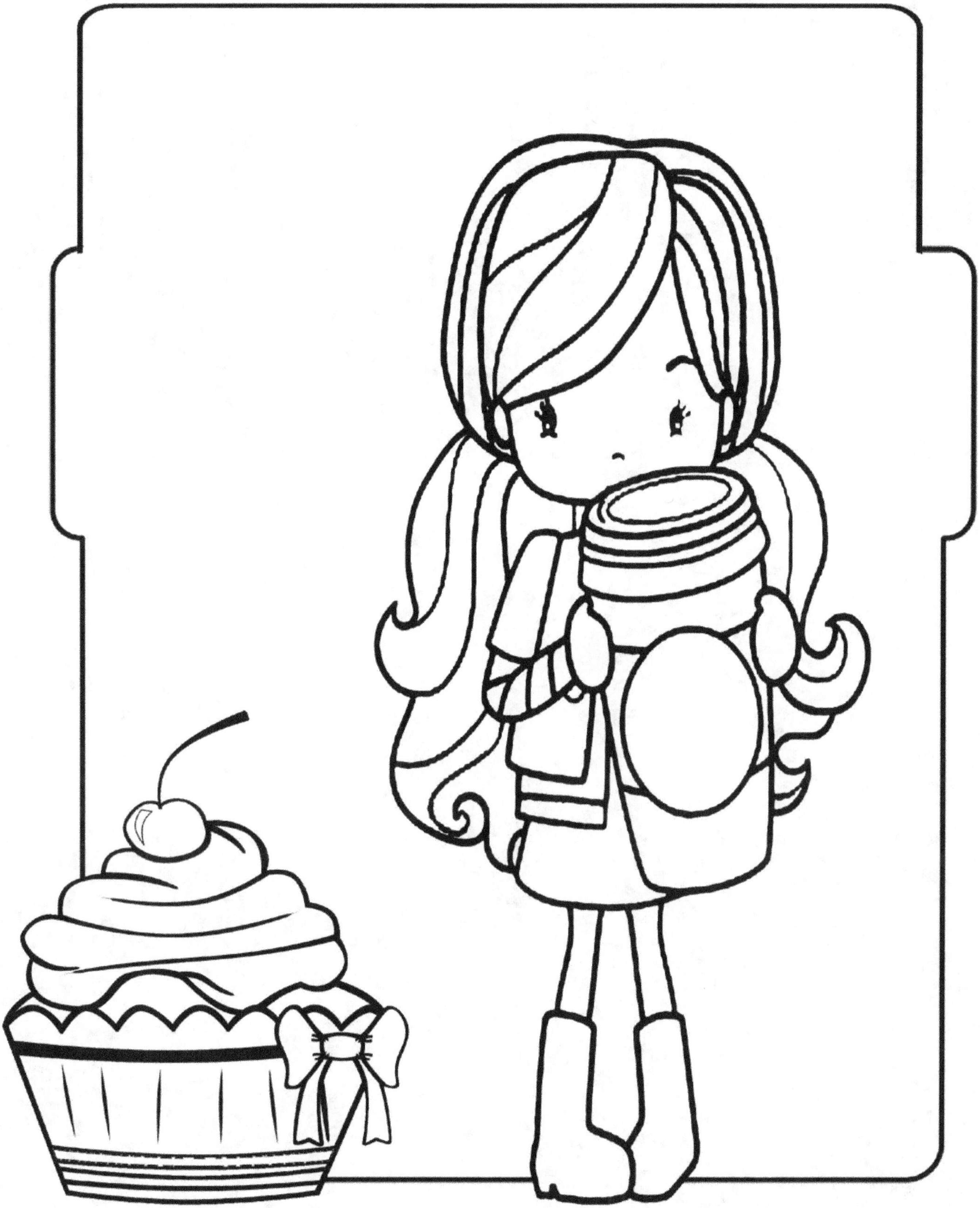

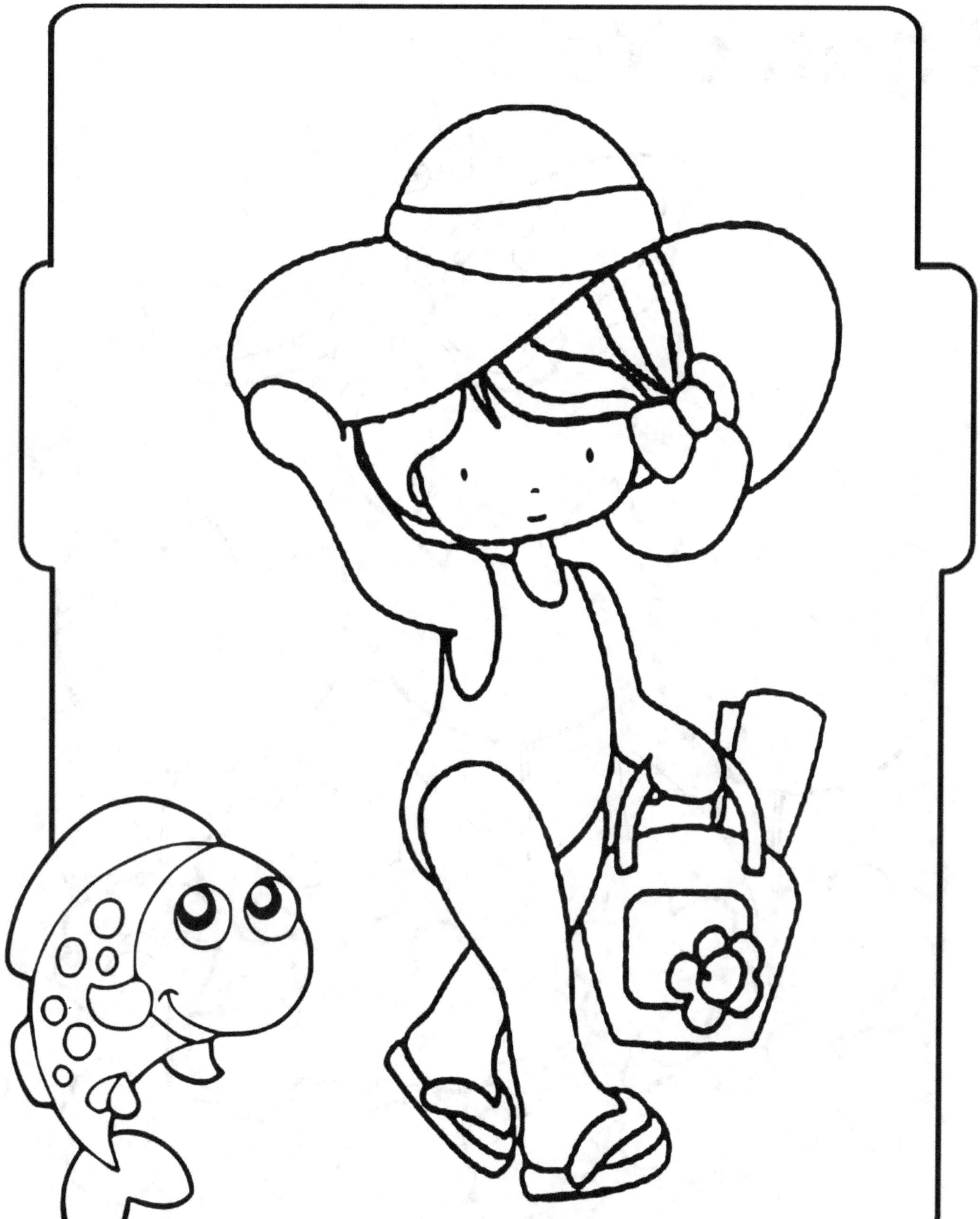

Thank You

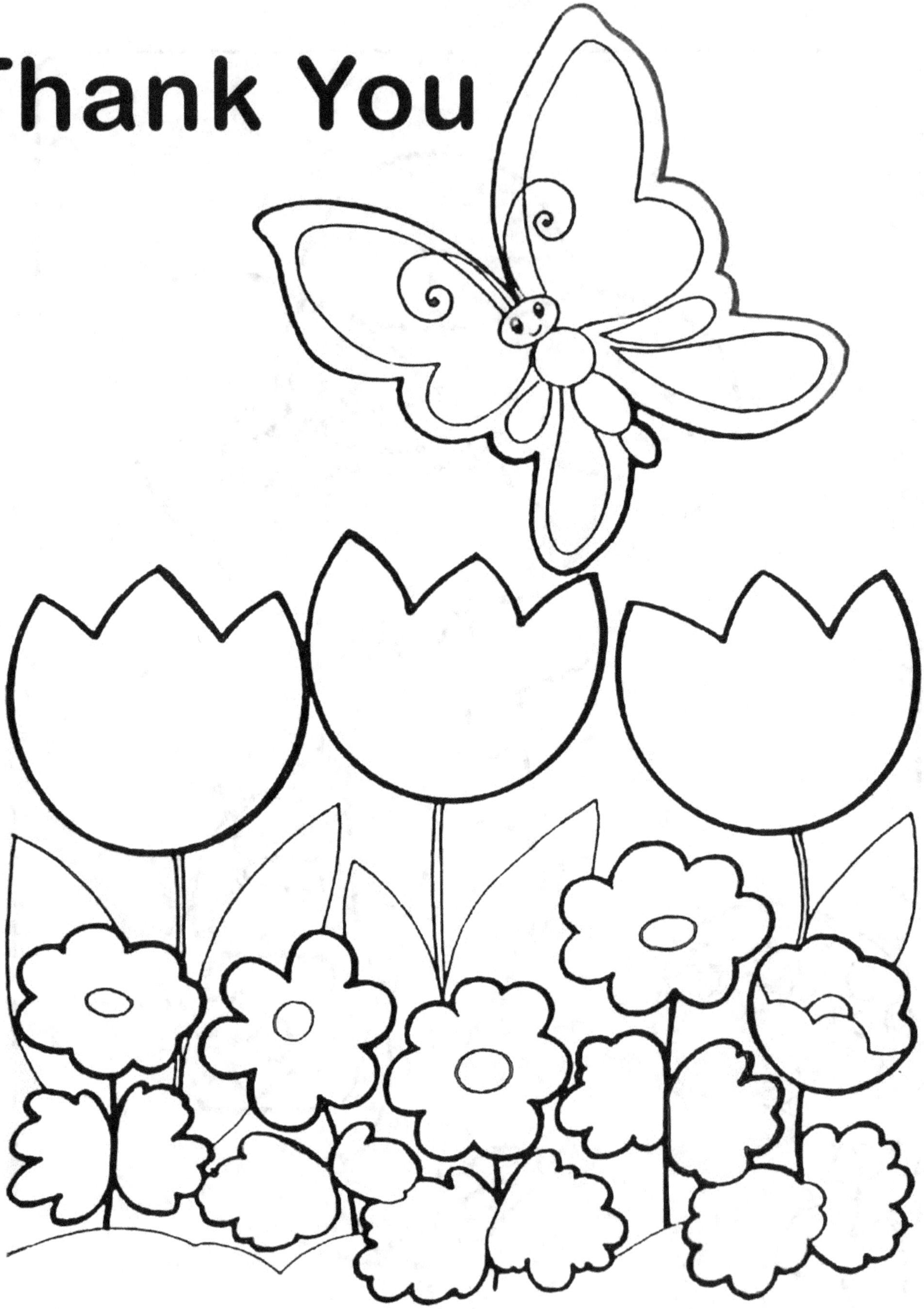

www.ingramcontent.com/pod-product-compliance
Lightning Source LLC
Chambersburg PA
CBHW081618220526
45468CB00010B/2925
* 9 7 8 1 9 8 4 9 8 0 6 8 7 *